2 CORINTHIANS

WORD and SPIRIT COMMENTARY ON THE NEW TESTAMENT

2 CORINTHIANS

Ben Witherington III

Baker Academic
a division of Baker Publishing Group
Grand Rapids, Michigan

© 2024 by Ben Witherington III

Published by Baker Academic
a division of Baker Publishing Group
Grand Rapids, Michigan
BakerAcademic.com

Printed in the United States of America

Library of Congress Cataloging-in-Publication Data
Names: Witherington, Ben, III, 1951– author.
Title: 2 Corinthians / Ben Witherington III.
Other titles: Second Corinthians
Description: Grand Rapids, Michigan : Baker Academic, a division of Baker Publishing Group,
    [2024] | Series: Word and spirit commentary on the New Testament | Includes bibliographical
    references and index.
Identifiers: LCCN 2024004939 | ISBN 9781540967466 (paperback) | ISBN 9781540968470
    (casebound) | ISBN 9781493448418 (ebook) | ISBN 9781493448425 (pdf)
Subjects: LCSH: Bible. Corinthians, 2nd—Commentaries.
Classification: LCC BS2675.53 .W58 2024 | DDC 227/.207—dc23/eng/20240320
LC record available at https://lccn.loc.gov/2024004939

Unless otherwise indicated, Scripture quotations are the author's own translation.

Scripture quotations labeled NIV taken from the Holy Bible, New International Version®, NIV®. Copyright © 1973, 1978, 1984, 2011 by Biblica, Inc.® Used by permission of Zondervan. All rights reserved worldwide. www.zondervan.com. The "NIV" and "New International Version" are trademarks registered in the United States Patent and Trademark Office by Biblica, Inc.®

24   25   26   27   28   29   30   7   6   5   4   3   2   1

Contents

Series Preface

In the foreword to Roger Stronstad's 1984 volume *The Charismatic Theology of St. Luke*, Clark H. Pinnock wrote, "The young Pentecostal scholars are coming!"[1] That was a generation ago, and now the pentecostal scholars are here, many of them having grown up alongside the explosive global growth of charismatic and pentecostal traditions. Such growth has been well documented,[2] with the number of adherents estimated at more than half a billion. In many places, Bible teaching has not been able to keep pace with this growth. Because of this reality, there is a clear need for a balanced commentary series aimed at Christians who identify as Spirit-filled, including renewalists, charismatics, and pentecostals, as well as others who want to learn more from this sphere of the church.

Because so many within these traditions often use wider evangelical literature, this series is sensitive to those intellectual and academic standards. However, others mistrust what they see as "purely intellectual" approaches, and they will find that this series also focuses on how the same Spirit who inspired the text speaks and works today. In this way the series offers a conversation for the church rather than operating primarily as a forum for discussion among scholars.

The commentary proper in each volume engages the biblical text both in its ancient setting and with regard to its message for Spirit-filled Christians

1. Clark H. Pinnock, foreword to *The Charismatic Theology of St. Luke*, by Roger Stronstad (Peabody, MA: Hendrickson, 1984), vii.

2. For example, Peter L. Berger, "Four Faces of Global Culture," in *Globalization and the Challenges of a New Century: A Reader*, ed. Patrick O'Meara, Howard D. Mehlinger, and Matthew Krain (Bloomington: Indiana University Press, 2000), 425; Robert Bruce Mullin, *A Short World History of Christianity* (Louisville: Westminster John Knox, 2008), 211 (cf. 276); Mark A. Noll, *The New Shape of World Christianity: How American Experience Reflects Global Faith* (Downers Grove, IL: IVP Academic, 2009), 32.

today. The commentaries often integrate exegesis and application, as readers in charismatic and pentecostal traditions tend to move naturally between these categories rather than separating them. In other words, such readers traditionally blend the ancient and modern horizons so as to read themselves within the continuing narrative of salvation history—that is, as part of the ongoing biblical story (not part of ancient culture but as theologically/spiritually/eschatologically part of God's same church).

As part of the blending of horizons, distinctive interests for Spirit-filled audiences are addressed when relevant. These include—but are not limited to—the reality of the new birth, healing and other miracles, spiritual gifts, hearing God's voice, the working of the Spirit in daily life, spiritual warfare, and so on. Not all biblical texts, and thus not all exposition, focuses on these points alone, and our authors do not artificially impose these topics on passages that do not naturally address them. In other words, our authors observe how God works in the biblical texts and how Christians can expect God to be working today, even if in new or culturally surprising ways.

However, each author also writes from within a charismatic, renewalist, or pentecostal context across the broad spectrum of the Spirit-focused tradition, and the authors often refer to such spaces in their writing. The range of voices includes denominational Pentecostals, Reformed charismatics, charismatic Methodists, and others. They also reflect a range of cultures, including Spirit-filled voices from multiple continents.

The authors "preach" their way through the texts, hosting a conversation both as trusted insiders for their own home traditions and as hospitable guides for others who wish to listen again alongside the ancient audiences for the Spirit's voice in our time and contexts. The commentaries are written with other distinctives of the tradition(s), including the incorporation of testimony and sidebars that feature connections to pentecostal/charismatic/revival history, teaching, and practice.

Other sidebars focus on biblical background and lengthier points of application. The series has adopted the NIV as the default text, as it is widely used in contexts that identify as Spirit-filled. However, our authors will often reference other translations, including their own. Quoted biblical texts from the passage under discussion will be highlighted in bold. Greek words are transliterated.

We offer this series to the church, and we pray that it testifies to the creative work and restorative goodness of the triune God.

Holly Beers, Westmont College
Craig S. Keener, Asbury Theological Seminary

Preface

Thirty years ago, I launched a series of socio-rhetorical commentaries on the books of the New Testament, the first of which was *Conflict and Community in Corinth* (1995). This commentary will be quite different from that one, not least because I will be drawing on resources that have emerged since that commentary appeared or that were not dealt with in that commentary. In short, this is a fresh look at 2 Corinthians, and from a mostly different perspective using different resources.

I wish to thank my Asbury colleague Craig Keener and also Holly Beers for inviting me to write this commentary and to thank Baker Academic for agreeing to publish it. It is rare that a scholar gets a second bite at one of the most interesting, and one could say juiciest, apples in the New Testament. And juicy it is, full of passion and pain, joy and sorrow, angst and anger on page after page. My hope is that the reader will get a real sense of what moved Paul to write this document and why it is still moving us all today. As one of my beloved and now departed professors, Richard Lovelace at Gordon-Conwell, once said, the Word without the Spirit is like wineskins without the wine. But it is also true that the Spirit without the Word has nothing to contain it, give it shape, preserve it, and let it age well. We need not only to understand the Scriptures but also to live a good Christian life grounded in those Scriptures.

This commentary is dedicated to my old friends, now retired, Richard Hays, Richard Bauckham, and Tom Wright. Thanks for all the inspiration and encouragement over many decades.

Easter 2024

Abbreviations

Old Testament

Gen.	Genesis	2 Chron.	2 Chronicles	Dan.	Daniel
Exod.	Exodus	Ezra	Ezra	Hosea	Hosea
Lev.	Leviticus	Neh.	Nehemiah	Joel	Joel
Num.	Numbers	Esther	Esther	Amos	Amos
Deut.	Deuteronomy	Job	Job	Obad.	Obadiah
Josh.	Joshua	Ps(s).	Psalm(s)	Jon.	Jonah
Judg.	Judges	Prov.	Proverbs	Mic.	Micah
Ruth	Ruth	Eccles.	Ecclesiastes	Nah.	Nahum
1 Sam.	1 Samuel	Song	Song of Songs	Hab.	Habakkuk
2 Sam.	2 Samuel	Isa.	Isaiah	Zeph.	Zephaniah
1 Kings	1 Kings	Jer.	Jeremiah	Hag.	Haggai
2 Kings	2 Kings	Lam.	Lamentations	Zech.	Zechariah
1 Chron.	1 Chronicles	Ezek.	Ezekiel	Mal.	Malachi

New Testament

Matt.	Matthew	Eph.	Ephesians	Heb.	Hebrews
Mark	Mark	Phil.	Philippians	James	James
Luke	Luke	Col.	Colossians	1 Pet.	1 Peter
John	John	1 Thess.	1 Thessalonians	2 Pet.	2 Peter
Acts	Acts	2 Thess.	2 Thessalonians	1 John	1 John
Rom.	Romans	1 Tim.	1 Timothy	2 John	2 John
1 Cor.	1 Corinthians	2 Tim.	2 Timothy	3 John	3 John
2 Cor.	2 Corinthians	Titus	Titus	Jude	Jude
Gal.	Galatians	Philem.	Philemon	Rev.	Revelation

Deuterocanonical Works

2 Macc.	2 Maccabees	Wisd.	Wisdom of Solomon
Sir.	Sirach		

Old Testament Pseudepigrapha

Apoc. Mos.	Apocalypse of Moses	T. Levi	Testament of Levi
2 En.	2 Enoch		

Bible Versions

LXX	Septuagint	NRSV	New Revised Standard Version
NIV	New International Version		

Introduction

Our earliest manuscript of this Greek text, $\mathfrak{P}^{46}$, which dates to about AD 150 if not a bit earlier, has the heading in Greek, *Pros Korinthious B*, which in turn means that the person who added this header saw this document as a single document and, further, didn't know of any others written by Paul to the Corinthians other than the one called *Pros Korinthious A*, which is to say our 1 Corinthians.[1] That, however, is not the end of the story.

While 2 Corinthians is the second Pauline Corinthian document that we have in the New Testament, it is in fact in all likelihood the fourth document that Paul wrote to the Corinthians. The first is mentioned in 1 Cor. 5:9, where Paul refers to a letter written before our 1 Corinthians. And then in 2 Cor. 2:1–4 we hear about a severe or sorrowful letter, likely written prior to our 2 Corinthians. So, we know of at least four letters to Corinth once 2 Corinthians was written; and were that not enough, a large number of scholars think that 2 Corinthians itself is a composite document, involving at least chapters 1–9, on the one hand, and then chapters 10–13, a later composition.

Two things can be said in regard to this latter suggestion: (1) there is no textual evidence for 2 Cor. 10–13 being a separate document; (2) in any case, long discourses like our 2 Corinthians often were composed in stages, sometimes over many days, during which time more information may have arrived, with Paul taking into account the developing situation. In any case, Paul's longer letters sometimes do have digressions (e.g., see 1 Cor. 13; 2 Cor. 6:14–7:1). I have given reasons in my earlier commentary on 2 Corinthians why this document can be viewed as a rhetorical unity with some digressions, and that material does

---

1. See Long, *II Corinthians*, 1.

not need to be repeated here.[2] I will treat the document as a unity, though probably composed over a considerable period of time in the mid- to late AD 50s. Fortunately, there is really no debate about the authorship of 2 Corinthians. It is written by Paul in the midst of his ongoing and rather turbulent relationship with the Corinthians, probably from Macedonia, perhaps in particular from Philippi.

Lest we imagine that the impressive and rather comprehensive document that we call 1 Corinthians had solved all the ethical and theological and practical problems raised and addressed in that document, 2 Corinthians clearly shows otherwise. And here we have a useful reality check for us as pastors, laypersons, and Bible teachers today. We may have preached or taught our greatest sermon or lesson, and may have been under the impression that doing so solved the major dilemmas that the congregation faces, only to discover that *it is not so*. A diverse congregation involves diverse points of view, including diverse opinions about the pastor and his or her leadership style, ability, and communication skills. Alas, it has always been thus. If even as strong a personality as Paul of Tarsus can face the difficulties that we find him facing in both 1 Corinthians and 2 Corinthians, then we should not be at all surprised that we face similar dilemmas. And make no mistake: Paul is very much on the defensive in 2 Corinthians, hence its character and apologetic (in the sense of reasoned defense, not in the sense of the modern word "apologizing") tone.

Paul is hurt and angry; he has opponents who have bewitched, bothered, and bewildered the Corinthians whom he must critique; and he is not yet able to go to Corinth in person and sort things out. And a significant part of the problem is that these opponents are claiming to have better spiritual and rhetorical gifts and more spiritual authority, and they have resorted to the usual tactic of touting themselves at the expense of the absent apostle Paul. Paul's only resort at the moment is to write the discourse we know as 2 Corinthians, hand it to one of his coworkers, likely Timothy or Titus, and tell them to go and proclaim it to those contentious souls in Corinth. The good news this time is that it appears to have helped, because by the time Paul gets to writing the Letter to the Romans, he is in the eastern port city of Corinth known as Cenchreae. This is also the impression that one might get from a close reading of Acts 20:2–3.

But who are these opponents who have landed in Corinth and caused so much trouble for the apostle to the Gentiles? Scholars have made various conjectures, but what seems clear at this point is this: (1) they are Jews who claim to be followers of Christ, but not the sort of Judaizers demanding that Gentiles be circumcised such as Paul confronted in Galatia; (2) they are rhetorically skilled

---

2. See Witherington, *Conflict and Community*, 325–57; also Long, *II Corinthians*, xvii–xliii.

and are all too happy to tout their own verbal skills; (3) they are charismatics or pneumatics, who also tout their various spiritual gifts and experiences. Paul has to resort to some mock boasting about his own experiences, including a remarkable visionary experience (2 Cor. 12). It is important, then, to understand that Paul is frequently being ironic and deliberately but indirectly ridiculing the boasting of the opponents in Corinth, who seem to have arrived after Paul wrote 1 Corinthians.

In a sense, we owe these opponents a debt of thanks, since they provoked Paul into talking about some of his spiritual experiences that we otherwise would not have known about. In a sense, 2 Corinthians seems to have always been embroiled in controversy, like the Corinthian Christians themselves. The earliest personal witness to the existence of this letter in the postapostolic era is, unfortunately, Marcion, the heretic who claimed that 2 Corinthians was a genuine Pauline letter, part of his own truncated version of a New Testament, which he compiled sometime between AD 139 and 144, which in turn prompted Tertullian to critique Marcion's truncated canon, making polemical uses of 2 Cor. 3:6–18, 4:1–7, and 5:1–10 against him.[3]

As for the structure of 2 Corinthians, here is a brief outline:

1. The epistolary prescript, involving the addressor and addressees (1:1–2)
2. A blessing prayer or rhetorical introduction (1:3–7)
3. A narration of relevant facts and data that explain where the apostle is and why he has not visited again, after his painful visit, during which he was attacked (a visit that happened after the writing of 1 Corinthians and produced the "severe" letter) (1:8–2:16)
4. The basic proposition of Paul's defense that he is indeed their apostle despite his refusal to accept patronage (2:17)
5. Opening argument, part one: The appeal to the Old Testament and to the Corinthians themselves as living proof of his authentic ministry (3:1–18)
6. Opening argument, part two: Paul's ironic self-praise (4:1–5:10)
7. Opening argument, part three: Paul the persuading ambassador for Christ (5:11–6:2)
8. Opening argument, part four: The trials and tribulations of the apostle (6:3–13)
9. A digression about avoiding entangling alliances (6:14–7:1)
10. "As I was saying," concluding the previous argument with amplification: Joy and sorrow from Titus's report (7:2–16)

---

3. See the discussion in Thrall, *Second Epistle to the Corinthians*, 1:3.

11. Argument two: "Now, about the collection" (8:1–9:15)

12. Argument three, part one: Dueling ministries (10:1–18)

13. Argument three, part two: The fool's discourse (11:1–12:10)

14. Argument three, part three: Parting shots—refusing to be a peddler of God's Word (12:11–13:4)

15. The peroration: The last harangue—the defense rests (13:5–10)

16. Closing greetings and remarks (13:11–14)[4]

Corinth in Historical Context

Corinth was a seaport town, indeed a double seaport town, with one port facing the Aegean and one facing the Adriatic, and it partook of all the sorts of features that such a town had. There were many transients passing through the town on the way east or west, lots of merchants shipping goods in both directions, and small boats were even being dragged across the little spit of land north of Corinth at the isthmus to avoid the long and dangerous journey around southern Greece. With all this trade coming and going, Corinth was a growing town, and the Romans realized that it would be best to make it the capital of the province of Achaia, something that no doubt irritated those living in Athens to no end.

The Romans had conquered the Greek city of Corinth in the second century BC and in due course had made it a Roman colony city. But what did that entail? A Roman colony city was a place where Rome mustered out various of its soldiers from various of its wars as it expanded its empire from west to east. They couldn't all come home to Rome, and in any case many of them were not Romans by birth but rather auxiliaries who were given Roman citizenship for their service to the empire and a piece of land and a pension of sorts. But once a town underwent a Roman takeover, it became legally a miniature of Rome itself. Its laws were the laws of Rome, its upper echelon of society and leaders were Romans, and its official judicial language was Latin, even though there were surely more people in Corinth that spoke Greek than spoke Latin. Rome had realized that it would be smarter to piggyback on the Hellenistic revolution brought about by Alexander the Great, and so Greek was the everyday lingua franca, or common language, of the empire. This is in part why Paul's letters to the Corinthians are in Greek not Latin.

But Paul himself had an advantage over most of the Greeks who lived in Achaia. He was not only a Greek-speaking Jew; he was a Roman citizen. As

---

4. Cf. Long, *II Corinthians*, xix–xxii.

anyone who has studied ancient Roman law knows, the Roman law favored Roman citizens, and so it is in no way surprising that the proconsul Gallio, who didn't much like Jews and was the governor of that province for only a couple of years, threw out the charges against Paul as brought by members of the local synagogue (see the story as told in Acts 18:12–17). Not incidentally, the mention of Gallio is crucial to our figuring out when Paul was where, because if he went on trial before Gallio, this surely had to have happened about AD 51, when we know that Gallio was there according to an interesting inscription up the mountain at Delphi where the oracle was.

Another thing we learn is that Paul did not operate like a modern evangelistic preacher. Notice that according to Acts 18, Paul stayed in Corinth for more than a year and a half initially and then returned there several times. He operated more like a missionary church planter than an itinerant evangelist. We also learn from Acts 18 that Paul was a leatherworker.

Leatherworking could involve making wineskins, sandals, satchels, and, of course, tents. We are told that Paul did the latter in Corinth with two other Christians who became his coworkers, Priscilla and Aquila. Because Corinth celebrated the Isthmian Games every two years (which means that in all likelihood Paul was present for one such celebration), there was a regular need for tents for those attending. Paul practiced this trade when he needed to, but as 1 Cor. 9 makes plain, he believed that he should be paid for his work for the gospel, where it did not involve patronage, and so he gladly accepted funds from the Philippians while he was in Corinth. In Corinth there were too many high-status persons who wanted to turn Paul into their client and in-house after-dinner speaker, something that Paul refused, which miffed various of the Corinthians who had become Christians. Patrons and clients made the economic world go around, and Paul's refusal to play the game upset people.

If we ask the question of how, exactly, a devout Pharisaic Jew became a Roman citizen, the leatherworking trade likely provides the clue. Paul was from Tarsus, a major city of importance to the Romans, near which there was a Roman legion encamped. Paul's family made tents out of the local goat's hair cloth, called *cilicium*, after the region's name, Cilicia. It is likely that Paul's father and family were granted Roman citizenship for their service to the local Roman legion. In fact, Acts 22:23–30 tells us that Paul was born a Roman citizen. Paul, however, didn't disclose this fact except when necessary, and when it gave him a legal advantage in Philippi, in Corinth, in Jerusalem, and on the way to and in Rome. In fact, Paul never directly mentions the fact in his letters. Why not?

The likely answer is that Paul did not want the gospel to be accepted because of the social status of its proclaimer. He wanted it to be embraced on its own merits by persuasion, not by a sense of obligation or coercion. As Paul says, he wanted to offer the gospel to one and all, free of charge, from those at the top of the social hierarchy to those at the bottom, slaves. The good news was for everyone. The other reason we do not hear about Paul's Roman citizenship in his letters is that all are written to people who are *already* Christians, at least ostensibly so, and Paul's authority over them has to do with his being their apostle, the one who brought them the gospel of Christ, by which they became new creatures, changed persons. Paul would not play his Roman citizenship trump card with them, because they already had accepted him as a different kind of authority figure, a religious authority figure like a priest or the oracle at Delphi, since Paul spoke prophecies (see 1 Cor. 14). We must keep these things in mind when we read 2 Corinthians.[5]

Recent Research on 2 Corinthians

It has been encouraging, since I published my first Corinthians commentary, to see not only how many fresh and interesting commentaries have been done on 2 Corinthians, but also how many monographs and articles have in fact argued for the unity of this discourse, and quite a few of them not from a rhetorical analysis point of view. For example, Christopher Land, in *The Integrity of 2 Corinthians and Paul's Aggravating Absence*, using a theoretically motivated and comprehensive approach, is able to conclude firmly that all this material in 2 Corinthians belongs together as one letter. He concludes that 2 Corinthians shows all the appearances of being a single text and should be reexamined accordingly.[6] This is also the judgment found in the majority of recent commentaries and monographs, many of them excellent, on 2 Corinthians.[7] Gone are the days when we find a majority of scholars advocating partition theories or that Paul is combating Gnosticism and Gnostics in Corinth.[8] Second Corinthians at least presents the so-called super-apostles as charismatic Jews who claim to be Christians, like Paul, not Gentiles at all. And yes, there is also still plenty of traditional historical-critical exegesis of the text in detail, for example the landmark work in the International Critical

5. For much more of this sort of information, besides consulting Witherington, *Conflict and Community*, see Witherington, *The Paul Quest*.
6. Land, *Integrity of 2 Corinthians*. And from a historical-rhetorical point of view, see Long, *Ancient Rhetoric and Paul's Apology*; cf. Vegge, *2 Corinthians*.
7. See, e.g., the work of P. Barnett, L. Belleville, R. Collins, F. Danker, D. Garland, G. Guthrie, S. Hafemann, M. Harris, J. Lambrecht, C. Keener, F. Matera, J. McCant, J. Scott, M. Seifrid, and T. D. Stegman.
8. Here I am talking about the majority of scholars who have written something on 2 Corinthians since 1995.

Commentary series by Margaret Thrall, done in two volumes in 1994 and 2004.[9]

The best of the small commentaries on both 1 and 2 Corinthians is Craig Keener's volume in the New Cambridge Bible Commentary series.[10] He offers a lot of good rhetorical analysis, and analysis in general in terms of the relevant Jewish and Greco-Roman literature of that period of history. The volume is full of careful exegesis and lots of new insights about the context as well as the content of 2 Corinthians.

There has also been the sort of rhetorical analysis pioneered by Vernon Robbins that involves both ancient and modern rhetorical analysis, with the use of Robbins's categories—for instance, inner texture, sacred texture, and more. In 2016 B. J. Oropeza published a massive commentary on 2 Corinthians in a Society of Biblical Literature series, following that approach.[11] The difficulty with it is that there are so many subcategories of textures that one finds oneself dealing with the same portion of text over and over again as parceled out to these different modern categories, categories that Paul did not use. It can be debated whether those categories can actually be derived from or suit the ancient text itself. Nevertheless, there is a huge amount of valuable and fresh discussion of the text in Oropeza's commentary.

More helpful is the commentary by Frank Matera from within the Catholic tradition, taking into account much of the recent discussion in Europe, particularly Germany. Matera argues for the unity of the whole letter, while arguing that this is perhaps Paul's most personal and revealing letter.[12] "In terms of content, it deals with the nature and exercise of Paul's apostolic ministry, functioning as a kind of *apologia pro vita sua* [apology or defense for your life]. In terms of tone, it is both compassionate and defensive, reconciling and provocative, forgiving and threatening, joyful and complaining, as Paul expresses his love for as well as his disappointment with a community that has misunderstood the nature of his ministry among them."[13]

Both Murray Harris and George Guthrie have produced fine, detailed, large commentaries on 2 Corinthians of a traditional historical-exegetical sort, but of the two, Guthrie is the one who takes into account again and again the rhetorical character of the letter, while Harris sticks to more traditional sorts of contextual exegesis. David Garland has also produced an excellent commentary that is more

9. Thrall, *Second Epistle to the Corinthians*.
10. Keener, *1–2 Corinthians*.
11. Oropeza, *Exploring Second Corinthians*.
12. N. T. Wright has suggested that this letter is more pastoral than even the Pastoral Epistles, and I think he is right.
13. Matera, *II Corinthians*, 1.

readable than some of the larger exegetical volumes on 2 Corinthians. In addition, we can now mention Finny Philip's dissertation under J. D. G. Dunn, published in 2005 as *The Origins of Pauline Pneumatology*, and J. Ayodeji Adewuya's *Holiness in the Letters of Paul*, published in 2016. The latter is particularly helpful in dealing with Paul's discussion of both the process of sanctification and also the ethical demands that are based on the internal renovating that the Spirit does in a person's life. I will say more about this important study in the commentary itself.

This is only a small sampling of what has been written in the last twenty-five or so years on this Pauline letter, and it can be said, obviously, that 2 Corinthians proves to continue to be a challenging and fruitful field for further digging and probing. The text has by no means given up all of its treasures yet.

Perhaps the most thoughtful recent presentation of the unity of 2 Corinthians that takes into account all the major possibilities is found in George Guthrie's recent commentary on this book.[14] Guthrie rightly thinks that the discourse reflects the relational tensions and back-and-forth of Paul's stormy interaction with the Corinthians. What Paul is doing in 2 Corinthians is carefully addressing various aspects of the relationship, leaving perhaps the most difficult aspect, the interfering false teachers who are there, until last.

One approach that is not helpful when studying 2 Corinthians is the charting of apparent chiasms (A-B-B-A structure, for instance) in the text. Why not? A chiasm of any length at all is a *visual* structure—it has to be seen to be appreciated—but 2 Corinthians, like all such discourses or even letters, is an oral and aural document meant to be heard, not carefully looked at. The literacy rate of perhaps 15 percent in the Greco-Roman world meant that if information was going to be conveyed to a group that involved a significant number of nonliterate persons, the document needed to be read out to them; and not only so, it would be read out seriatim, whether a letter or discourse. What I mean by this is that one could not know that a chiasm was coming by hearing the document in the order in which it was written. One would not know that the A would be followed in due course by an A′ or that the B that followed the A would be followed by a B′, much less that there might be a center to that structure, C, which was the key to understanding the A and B. Oral cultures were not geared to find such structures on the fly when they had simply heard the document straight through, not read it. Perhaps a very tight A-B-B-A structure involving a few verses could register, but only after the whole of it had been heard. But that is not the case with a lengthy chiastic structure.[15]

---

14. Guthrie, *2 Corinthians*, 23–50.

15. Nevertheless, commentators still try to find chiasms in documents such as 2 Corinthians. See, e.g., Garland, *2 Corinthians*, 422–23. I am apt to say that such structures come from the mind of the beholder.

How to Read a Complex Rhetorical Discourse

Unfortunately, we live in an age, partly due to the advances in technology, when we have been conditioned to expect everything to be quick, easy to understand and handle, readily available to be processed quickly. We have fast food, fast internet, fast cars, fast refunds—I could go on. And this expectation has invaded the church as well. Preachers have talked about the KISS principle ("Keep it simple, stupid"), or putting the cookies on the bottom shelf where all can reach them, or distilling everything down to an eighth-grade level of vocabulary and understanding. Paul, however, did not live in such a world, and his 2 Corinthians is complex, and requires one to do what C. H. Dodd once said that Jesus' parables require: one must tease one's mind into active thought, and really concentrate. This is all the more the case given that 2 Corinthians is full of complex ethical and theological ideas and has a rhetorical structure that those who know nothing about rhetoric will not recognize easily or understand because they have never seriously studied ancient rhetorical discourse structures.

Perhaps the most important thing one can say is that this material should not be sound-bited, or chopped up into small, bite-size chunks. Why? Because for one thing, what we have is a continuous argument in various parts from 2 Cor. 3:1–7:16 with one digression from the main discussion. And within that lengthy argument we have all sorts of colorful metaphors, images, and ideas that assume that the audience will know something about defense speeches, about Roman triumphs, about reciprocity and ancient patronage relationships, about ambassadors of rulers, and much more. Furthermore, some of the main problems that Paul is actually confronting and addressing do not come fully to light until 2 Cor. 10–13.

In short, this document needs to be studied carefully in its original contexts, or as I like to say, "A text without a context is just a pretext for whatever you want it to say." And, frankly, it does a disservice to both the Word and the Spirit (never mind to the apostle himself) to fail to do one's homework and to do the necessary contextual study and rumination on the discourse's depths, instead of cherry-picking this verse or that verse to teach or preach, and ending up reading things into the text that are simply not there, and calling it "the guidance of the Holy Spirit," when in fact it's the product of an overheated imagination that has not really come to grips with the depth and substance of the text.

I once had a student who was frustrated with all the reading and language work required in one of my exegesis classes on Paul, and I could tell he was upset. So, I asked him what was bothering him. His reply was a classic: "I don't know why I have to learn all this contextual stuff and study so hard when I can just get up in the pulpit and the Spirit will give me utterance." My reply was, "Yes, you can do that, but it is a shame you're not giving the Spirit more to work with."

In-depth study of this profound, emotional, rhetorical discourse full of ideas and pathos leads one to see Paul more clearly, understand the gospel better, and more deeply appreciate what the apostle of the Gentiles was prepared to do and to suffer for Christ, even when the opposition was multifaceted. Even within his Corinthian house churches he had doubters and detractors, never mind invasive false teachers. I urge one and all: take time to carefully work through 2 Corinthians and savor its flavor and substance. It will pay dividends and draw you closer to the Lord with a better understanding of the gospel.

It was John Donne, one of the greatest English poets and preachers ever, who preached at St. Paul's Cathedral in London, who once said, "Wheresoever I open St. Paul's letters I hear thunder, a thunder that resounds throughout the earth." History has proved him right. There is perhaps no letter of Paul that has more thunder and lightning (or as our German friends would say, *Sturm und Drang*, "storm and stress") than 2 Corinthians. It will require our careful and detailed attention to see exactly how this work speaks today, and how it may be used for the glorification of God and the edification of his people today. So, to the text itself we must now turn.

Recommended Resources

Garland, David E. *2 Corinthians*. New American Commentary 29. Nashville: Broadman & Holman, 1999.

Guthrie, George H. *2 Corinthians*. Baker Exegetical Commentary on the New Testament. Grand Rapids: Baker Academic, 2015.

Harris, Murray J. *The Second Epistle to the Corinthians: A Commentary on the Greek Text*. New International Greek Testament Commentary. Grand Rapids: Eerdmans, 2005.

Keener, Craig S. *1–2 Corinthians*. New Cambridge Bible Commentary. Cambridge: Cambridge University Press, 2005.

Kruse, Colin. *2 Corinthians*. Exegetical Guide to the Greek New Testament. Nashville: B&H Academic, 2020.

Lightfoot, J. B. *The Epistles of 2 Corinthians and 1 Peter: Newly Discovered Commentaries*. Edited by Ben Witherington III and Todd D. Still. Lightfoot Legacy Set 3. Downers Grove, IL: IVP Academic, 2016.

Long, Fredrick J. *II Corinthians: A Handbook on the Greek Text*. Baylor Handbook on the Greek New Testament. Waco: Baylor University Press, 2015.

Martin, Ralph P. *2 Corinthians*. 2nd ed. Word Biblical Commentary 40. Grand Rapids: Zondervan, 2014.

Matera, Frank J. *II Corinthians: A Commentary*. New Testament Library. Louisville: Westminster John Knox, 2003.

Oropeza, B. J. *Exploring Second Corinthians: Death and Life, Hardship and Rivalry*. Rhetoric of Religious Antiquity 3. Atlanta: SBL Press, 2016.

Thrall, Margaret E. *A Critical and Exegetical Commentary on the Second Epistle to the Corinthians*. 2 vols. International Critical Commentary. London: T&T Clark International, 1994–2004.

Witherington, Ben, III. *Conflict and Community in Corinth: A Socio-rhetorical Commentary on 1 and 2 Corinthians*. Grand Rapids: Eerdmans, 1995. [For a full list of valuable older commentaries on 2 Corinthians, see the bibliography in this earlier volume.]

Wright, N. T. *Paul for Everyone: 2 Corinthians*. 2nd ed. New Testament for Everyone. Louisville: Westminster John Knox, 2004.

The Epistolary Prescript

> **1:1Paul, an apostle of Christ Jesus through the will of God, and Timothy the brother, to the assembly of God that is in Corinth, together with all God's people in Achaia. 2Grace to you and peace from God our Father and the Lord Jesus Christ.[1]**

In a normal ancient letter opening there would simply be the name of the addressor and the name of the person or persons to whom the letter was sent with a simple greeting, like *Vale* ("Hail"), and perhaps a health wish (see Seneca, *Moral Epistles* 15.1). Paul, and other early Christians, modified such an opening such that Paul mentions up front his credentials or authority and where it comes from: he is an **apostle of Christ Jesus** by **the will of God**. It becomes apparent why he finds it necessary to offer this early on, as there were those among his opponents who were questioning if he even was an apostle, not least because he did not operate like other authority figures, who accepted patronage and worked within the existing reciprocity structure of the Greco-Roman world.

Paul, by contrast, refuses pay from the Corinthians because he does not want to become some wealthy Corinthian's client and be indebted to such a person, and also because he wants to offer the gospel free of charge. We learn later in 2 Cor. 8–9 and in Philippians that Paul is fine with "giving and receiving"—that is, a parity relationship like he has with the Philippians that doesn't involve his becoming subordinate to and a client of someone. Paul believes that "a workman is worthy of his hire" (see 1 Tim. 5:18), *but* in Corinth he refuses pay and works

---

1. All translations from the Greek of 2 Corinthians are my own. Special thanks go to Colin Kruse's work, which helped me with the translation.

at leatherworking because of the entangling alliances and obligations that are expected of him in that Roman colony city. Notice as well that this letter is also from **Timothy**, who is with Paul when it is written, though we may be sure that the main voice speaking in this document is Paul's. Timothy is just greeting a congregation that he knows or knows about.

The addressee in this case is not just the **assembly** [*ekklēsia*] **of God in Corinth**, but **all** the Christians **in Achaia**, the province of which Corinth is now the capital, where the governor lives. The word *ekklēsia*, which we often translate as "church," is actually not a technical term for a Christian assembly; in fact, in the golden age of Greece it was the word used for the democratic assembly that met in Athens, and then in the Greek Old Testament it was a term for the coming together of God's people for some purpose such as worship or teaching. It translates the Hebrew word *qahal*. N. T. Wright correctly notes that if we compare this opening with that of 1 Corinthians, only Corinth is mentioned there, but here, in the two or more years since the writing of 1 Corinthians, the gospel has spread elsewhere in the province of Achaia.[2]

Nine times Paul uses the term *ekklēsia* for his congregations in various places, and it occurs one hundred times in the Greek Old Testament. The point to make here is that the word would not be seen by either Jews or Greeks as a technical term for "the church," and if the majority of the audience were non-Jews, the resonance of the word would recall how it was used in Athens in the golden age of Greece, when a fledgling democracy would meet and discuss and debate policy and orators would try to persuade others to adopt this policy or that law. In short, the term would have a political resonance as well as a religious one, especially so because Paul mentions the Christians in the whole Roman province of Achaia. It should also be stressed that sometimes the phrase "the assembly of God" refers to what we would call the church in general, not one specific local congregation. This seems clear enough from 1 Cor. 15:9, Gal. 1:13, and Phil. 3:6, if not from a few other cases. Paul does not think that the "church" simply consists of a lot of separate congregations with no connection between them.

The people of God, in Paul's view, are Jew and Gentile united in Christ, an entity that Paul does not equate with "the Israel of God" (cf. Gal. 6:16). God has not abandoned Israel or reneged on his promises to them, but he intends to fulfill those promises in Christ. It is very clear from Rom. 9–11 that the term "Israel" refers to non-Christian Jews, and Paul sees them as having a future when Christ returns and "turns away the impiety of Jacob" (Rom. 11:26). Their future is not separate from the *ekklēsia*, as Paul says there that they will be saved "in the same manner" as the Gentiles, by grace through faith in Christ. At the eschaton,

2. Wright, *Paul for Everyone: 2 Corinthians*, 3.

Patrons and Clients in the Ancient World

In a world well before there was such a thing as free-market capitalism, and before there was any sort of level playing field in the ancient economy, the way things worked was that there were wealthy patrons and needy clients who had to come to patrons for help to get things done, including buying or selling land, starting a business, running for a political office, and much more. This is what scholars call a reciprocity system, or as we might call it, "You scratch my back, and I'll scratch yours." The problem for clients once they got into a reciprocity cycle was that it could become impossible to get out of it, unless the patron terminated the relationship. And furthermore, patrons almost never engaged with clients out of altruistic motives. There were always strings attached to the relationship. For example, if some patron was running for office, then it was the client's obligation to praise him to whomever he encountered, possibly even providing graffiti advertising on city walls about his patron being the best candidate for city treasurer, for example. We have found some of these sorts of ads on the walls at Pompeii.

For Paul, the reason for choosing to make leather goods with Priscilla and Aquila in Corinth was to avoid patronage with its possible ongoing obligations. For example, Paul could have been engaged by a patron to be an after-dinner speaker or rhetor at a banquet held by the patron during the part of the meal called the "symposium." But Paul wanted to offer the gospel free of charge, and he didn't want to be presented as a speaker for hire.

There were, however, parity relationships possible, called "giving and receiving" relationships, and in those sorts of relationships Paul was happy to receive money for support of his missionary work, and for the collection for Jerusalem from the Philippians and others. So, what we do not have in Corinth is Paul committing himself to what later came to be called "tentmaking" ministries, where one had to raise one's own support for a mission. Rather, Paul is trying to avoid patronage in Corinth, but this did not seem to be a problem if the relationship was not configured as a patron-client relation, whether with the Philippians or with someone like Phoebe in Cenchreae (see Rom. 16:1–4).[a]

a. For more on all this, see Witherington, *Conflict and Community*, and at a more popular level, Witherington, *Week in the Life of Corinth*.

BIBLICAL BACKGROUND

What Is a Roman Colony City?

When the Romans conquered various cities in Greece and farther east, some of them they converted into Roman colony cities, where Roman soldiers were mustered out and given land, and where a Roman structure of law and government was set up, with Romans running the courts and the government. Corinth had been such a city for more than a century by the time Paul got there in the AD 50s, and that provided him with a considerable advantage when he was taken to court there by Jewish officials, because he was a Roman citizen (see Acts 18). In fact, the Romans had made Corinth, not Athens, the capital city of the whole province of Achaia, not least because it was a growing double port town with lots of resources. Roman law always favored Roman citizens, even in colony cities like Corinth.

the non-Christian Jews, who were temporarily broken off from the people of God, will be reintegrated into the people of God, and in that manner "all Israel will be saved." In Paul's view there are not two peoples of God at any point in human history, and in the end there will only be one, which is "in Christ."[3]

In verse 2, as elsewhere in Paul's letters, he has modified the traditional Greek word for greeting, *chaire*, and instead uses *charis*, a cognate term meaning "grace" or "grace gift" in a theological sense. He then adds the traditional Jewish greeting of *shalom*, or in Greek *eirēnē*, "peace." To this he adds the explanation that this greeting is not just from himself and Timothy, but actually is from God the Father and the Lord Jesus. This signals that this letter conveys information and inspiration not just from the apostle but from God; it is the Word of God in the words of human beings.

It is interesting that wherever Paul actually uses the phrase "the Word of God," what he is referring to is his oral proclamation of the gospel, which changed the lives of his converts (see, e.g., 1 Thess. 2:13). It is not merely Paul's opinions as an authority figure. Paul sees himself as an inspired spokesman, indeed an authorized ambassador for God and Christ, such that his words carry a divine authority and operate as a change agent in human lives along with the work of the Holy Spirit, who convicts, convinces, and applies the Word in those lives.

3. On this, see the longer discussion in Thrall, *Second Epistle to the Corinthians*, 1:89–93; also Witherington, *Paul's Letter to the Romans*.

In fact, a close reading of 1 Cor. 7 shows that Paul does not distinguish between the authority of his own teachings and those of Christ; both are God's Word spoken. There is really no excuse for treating Paul's words as some sort of second-rate authority for Christian belief and behavior. As Paul says clearly enough in 1 Cor. 7:40, he also has the same Spirit of God who inspired God's earlier prophets, and Jesus Christ himself.

A Blessing Prayer / Rhetorical Introduction

> [1:3]Blessed be the God and Father of our Lord Jesus Christ, the Father of mercies and the God of all comfort. [4]He comforts us in all our afflictions so that we may be able to comfort those who are in any kind of affliction through the comfort we ourselves receive from God; [5]for just as the sufferings of Christ overflow unto us, so also through Christ our comfort overflows. [6]If we are afflicted, it is for your comfort and salvation. If we are comforted, it is for your comfort, which produces in you patient endurance of the same sufferings we suffer. [7]And our hope for you is firm, because we know that just as you share in our suffering, so also you will share in the comfort.

While it was customary to offer a health wish at the beginning or end of an ancient letter (e.g., "I hope this finds you well"), Paul expands this customary feature into a proper thanksgiving or, in this case, a blessing prayer with rich theological and ethical content. Paul is *not* thanking God *for* the suffering; he is blessing God for the comfort given in the midst of suffering. Nor is he thanking God here for the spiritual state of the Corinthians.[1] From the outset, Paul brings up the theme of his sufferings, and those of his audience, and he will have much more to say along these lines as the discourse progresses (cf. the catalog of sufferings in 11:21–31). A good deal of what Paul says about sufferings will have been counterintuitive to at least the Gentile portion of his audience. What good

---

1. Rightly, Keener, *1–2 Corinthians*, 157.

could possibly come from suffering, especially suffering caused by persecution for what one believes?

Paul knows that there are various kinds and sources of affliction, which is why he speaks of the diversity of such things. Certainly, Paul didn't believe that Christians, just because they have faith, even strong faith, would be exempt from all sorts of sufferings; indeed, he believed that a Christ-centered faith that was not merely a normal Jewish sort of faith, and was not recognized as a legitimate religion or faith by Rome, or for that matter a legitimate variant on Jewish faith by some of Paul's Jewish persecutors, was likely to produce suffering of various sorts. The relationship of genuine faith to suffering was complex, and often the former led to the latter. "Paul asserts that he shares the same divinely ordained paradox that 'constituted' the life and destiny of Jesus Christ: comfort from suffering, life from death, strength from weakness, and wisdom from foolishness (see 11:30; 12:5, 8–10; 13:2–9)."[2]

At the same time, notice how Paul says that God comforts him and his audience in all their sufferings. God is not viewed as *the source* of the suffering! He is viewed as the source of comfort in suffering, which God allows to happen but does not cause to happen. God's active role is in comforting the sufferer. This theme would be very familiar to any Jewish Christian in the audience, for Jews had endured persecution for many centuries, and many of them resonated with the word to the Babylonian exiles in Isa. 40:1: "Comfort, comfort my people, says your God." This comfort comes from God, even though much of their suffering had come about because of their own sins and unfaithfulness to God. The good news in Isa. 40 was that the time of suffering was completed, and it was now time to plan for the return to Zion.

It is very clear, if one reads the Corinthian correspondence and Romans closely, that Paul had long meditated on the message of Isa. 40–55 and reapplied some of it to himself and to his audience. At points he sees himself as like the suffering servant of Isa. 52–53, and he believes that his own suffering will benefit his converts, and the comfort he receives will flow over into his audience. Indeed, with Christ as *the* suffering servant of Isa. 52–53 in Paul's mind, he sees the sufferings of Christ himself flow over into his own life.

Elsewhere he can even talk about filling up the sufferings of Christ in his own body and experiences (Col. 1:24). So close is the relationship of this apostle to Christ that what happens to him happens to Christ, and what happens to the apostle is an extension of what happens to Christ. This theme of comfort predominates in 2 Corinthians more than in any other Pauline letter, indeed any other New Testament book (eleven occurrences of the term *paraklēsis* out of

---

2. Garland, *2 Corinthians*, 57.

twenty-nine in the entire New Testament). How very different this message of divine comfort must have sounded to former pagans who had heard the conventional sentiments expressed by Pliny the Elder: "That a supreme being, whatever it be, pays heed to human affairs is a ridiculous notion" (*Natural History* 2.5.20).[3]

This should remind us of the Pauline conversion scene in Acts 9, and how odd it appears on the surface when the heavenly Christ, who in that locale is immune to further physical suffering, says, "Saul, why are you persecuting me?" (9:4), referring to Saul's persecution of Christ's followers on earth. What Paul must have learned from that moment of divine intervention by Christ in his life is, "Inasmuch as you have done it unto the least of these, you have done it unto me" (Matt. 25:40). So Paul sees the sufferings of Christ flow over into his own life, but also the comfort of God, which then can flow over into the life of those he is addressing in 2 Corinthians, but only as they also patiently endure the same sufferings Paul is undergoing.

Notice especially the attempt by Paul to emphasize the close connection between him and his audience. His own comfort can flow over into his audience. There is a deep spiritual connection here. Notice as well that Paul's wise counsel is patient endurance of suffering, in his own case, but also in the case of his audience. The only exegetical issue here is this: Is Paul talking about comfort because of the suffering or about comfort producing the endurance during suffering?[4] The proper Christian response to suffering is neither retaliating against one's abusers nor railing against God, but rather following the example of the suffering servant—both the one in Isa. 53:7 (about whom it is said, "He was oppressed and afflicted, yet he did not open his mouth; he was led like a lamb to the slaughter, and as a sheep before its shearers is silent, so he did not open his mouth") and Christ himself, who prayed for his tormentors on the cross, "Father, forgive them, for they know not what they are doing" (Luke 23:34).

Now, this behavior is not natural. It is supernatural, made possible by the grace of God. Patient endurance of suffering, in some cases even suffering unto death, seems profoundly unnatural. Yet in these very sorts of circumstances Paul can speak of comfort, real comfort coming from God that makes it all endurable.

From a rhetorical point of view, this passage is meant to appeal to the audience's emotions and make them favorably disposed to hear what Paul will go on to say in the rest of this discourse. Paul is trying to reestablish rapport with his converts. The goal is to bind the audience more closely to Paul and to Christ and to wean them away from the false teachers or "super-apostles" who have been visiting the Corinthians and upsetting that relationship. So serious

---

3. Unless otherwise indicated, all translations of ancient texts are my own.
4. See Kruse, *2 Corinthians*, 16.

is this matter that Paul will have to resort to defending himself, defending his ministry, and contrasting with the self-centered aims of the opponents. He will use hyperbole and sarcasm and irony to cast shade on them and vindicate himself. Here it would be good to note that these practices, including highly emotive speech, were a common part of the Greco-Roman world. *These sorts of practices do not readily translate themselves to various, very different, modern Western cultures.* Lambasting people in your audience from the pulpit is not how you win people for Christ in our culture. I like to say, "If you want to win some, you need to be winsome, and persuade and love them into participation in the body of Christ."

This passage raises all sorts of profound questions for the modern pastor or lay leader of a church. For example, none of us are apostles in the Pauline sense (as opposed to just "sent ones" from a congregation, the so-called apostles commissioned by churches as opposed to those commissioned by the risen Christ himself). Apostles of the Pauline type are those who have seen the risen Lord during his initial appearances and been commissioned by him to be his servants and ambassadors. Do the practices and experiences of Paul really translate to those of modern church leaders? My short answer would be no, and in some limited respects, yes. First of all, if we are church planters and founders of congregations, humanly speaking, this does not make us apostles in the Pauline sense, nor does it make us authority figures who can speak or write Holy Scripture in the same way or to the same degree Paul did.

Yes, we can share comfort with God's people as Paul did, and share Pauline Scriptures with our audiences in very different circumstances. But we must not be under the delusion that we should bind our audience, in a cult-of-personality sort of way, to us as individual leaders. We may be inspired by the Spirit, but I would remind us all that Paul himself has warned us that we should speak according to the measure of our faith and not beyond it (Rom. 12:3) and use our gifts according to the measure of faith. As 1 Cor. 14 also makes abundantly clear, even prophetic speech must be sifted and weighed by the congregation, not simply taken as the latest Word from God, without careful reflection and critical examination. In other words, Paul has provided some guidelines for people like us, people like Timothy and Titus. We can model ourselves on Christ without developing a Messiah complex. We can model ourselves on Paul without developing an apostle complex or cultivating a cult of personality, which really is just something done to feed our own weak egos.

Finally, in regard to the issue of Christian suffering, Paul here is not talking in general about suffering caused by accidents, or disease, or anxieties over resources, or other sorts of mundane suffering. He is talking *specifically* about suffering that comes directly from serving Christ and bearing witness to him.

The Christocentric Character of 2 Corinthians

Even at a glance it becomes apparent that there are a lot of references to Christ in 2 Corinthians and not nearly as many references to the Holy Spirit. For instance, there is a strong emphasis on Paul's solidarity with Christ in his suffering (1:5; 4:10–11, 14; 8:9; 10:1; 12:10), and there is a lot of stress on Jesus as the exalted Lord (1:14; 2:14; 4:5, 14; 5:8, 10–11; 10:5, 8). There is, of course, some paradox here in that Christ is in heaven, and one might think that solidarity in suffering with Jesus doesn't make sense. However, from the experience of Paul on the Damascus road (Acts 9; 22; 26), we learn differently. Christ tells Saul (Paul) that persecuting Christ's followers is also persecuting Christ himself, so closely does Christ identify with his people. Equally interesting here at the beginning of 2 Corinthians, we are told in the same breath both that suffering draws one closer to Christ and that mercy and comfort come from the Father. The Father, the Son, and also the Spirit work together for the believer, but not infrequently they are portrayed as playing different roles. Whereas there is a strong emphasis on the Spirit in 1 Corinthians, in 2 Corinthians there is more of an emphasis on Christ, even to the point of his being the example to follow when it comes to generous giving for the collection, as we shall see in 2 Cor. 8:9.

So, in preaching or teaching this material we need to stick to the text, and not globalize the message to include all kinds of suffering of whatever source. And let me be clear that self-affliction, such as monks used to do with whips in the Middle Ages, is not commended by Paul, not least because you cannot atone for your own sins and do not need to do so, since Christ has already paid for them on the cross. When Paul speaks about "mortification of the flesh" (cf. Rom. 8:13; Gal. 5:24; Col. 3:5), he's talking about the stifling of the sinful inclinations, not the literal physical abusing of one's own body to no good end.

The Backstory

¹:⁸We do not wish you to be ignorant, brothers and sisters, of our affliction that happened in Asia. We were under great pressure, far beyond our ability to endure, so that we despaired of life itself. ⁹Indeed, we felt we had received in ourselves the sentence of death in order that we would trust not in ourselves but in the God who raises the dead, ¹⁰who has delivered us from a terrible death, and he will deliver us. On him we have set our hope that he will deliver us again, ¹¹with you joining in helping us with your prayers. Then many will give thanks on our behalf for the gracious favor granted us in answer to the prayers of many.

¹²For this is our boast, the witness of our conscience, that in the holiness and sincerity of God, not in mere human wisdom, by God's grace, we have conducted ourselves in the world, and especially so towards you, ¹³for we are writing nothing to you but what you can hear and comprehend. But I hope that you will understand fully, ¹⁴just as you have already understood in part, that we are your reason for boasting, just as you are ours in the day of our Lord Jesus. ¹⁵With this confidence, I planned to come to you first, so that you could have a second gift, ¹⁶and to visit you on my way to Macedonia and then come to you again from Macedonia and be sent on my way by you to Judea. ¹⁷Now, when I planned this, was I of two minds? Or what I plan do I plan according to the will of the flesh, so that I say yes indeed and no indeed at the same time? ¹⁸As God is faithful, our word to you is not yes and no, ¹⁹for the Son of God, Jesus Christ, whom we preached among you, through me and Silvanus and Timothy, did not become yes and no; to the contrary,

in him it is always yes! [20]For every one of God's promises is yes in him! Therefore, through him we say, "So be it, Amen," to the glory of God the Father.

[21]Now, God is the one who strengthens us together with you in Christ, and God who has anointed us. [22]He has even sealed us and as a down payment given us the Spirit in our hearts. [23]I call on God as a witness on my life that it was to spare you that I did not come to Corinth. [24]I do not mean that we lord it over your faith, but we are workers with you for your joy, because you stand firm in your faith.

[2:1]In fact, I made up my mind about this, that I would not come to you for another painful visit, [2]for if I cause you [more] pain, who will cheer me other than the one being hurt by me? [3]I wrote this very thing, so that when I came, I wouldn't have pain from those who ought to make me rejoice, because I am persuaded about all of you that my joy will be yours as well. [4]But I wrote to you with many tears out of great distress and an anguished heart, not to cause you pain, but that you should know the love I have for you. [5]If anyone has caused pain, he has caused pain not so much to me as in some measure—not to exaggerate—to all of you. [6]This punishment by the majority is sufficient for that person. [7]As a result, you should [now] forgive and comfort him, otherwise he may be overcome by excessive sorrow. [8]Therefore, I urge you to reaffirm your love to him. [9]I wrote [that severe/sorrowful letter] for this purpose: to test your character to see if you are obedient in all things. [10]Anyone you forgive, I do as well, for what I have forgiven, if I've forgiven anything, it is for your benefit in the presence of Christ, [11]so that we may not be taken advantage of by Satan, for we are not ignorant of his schemes.

[12]When I came to Troas to preach the gospel of Christ, even though the Lord opened the door for me, [13]I had no rest in my spirit because I did not find my brother Titus. Instead, I said goodbye to them and left for Macedonia. [14]But thanks be to God, who always leads us in Christ's triumphal procession, and through us spreads the aroma of the knowledge of him in every place. [15]For to God we are the fragrance of Christ among those who are being saved and among those who are perishing. [16]To some we are the aroma of death leading to death, but to others we are the aroma of life leading to life. Who is adequate for these things?

One of the regular debates among Pauline scholars is this: When Paul says "we," does he really mean "me," or is he talking about the views not only of himself but, in this case, also of Timothy and Silvanus, who are mentioned at the beginning of this letter? Here we are helped greatly by the greatest scholar of a previous generation, J. B. Lightfoot, and it will be well to share his views (see the sidebar "'I' and 'We' in 2 Corinthians and Elsewhere").

If we ask the question of why Paul would be so precise in this manner, the answer must in part come from his adherence to the Old Testament principle that to establish the truth of anything, it must be testified to by at least two witnesses (cf. Deut. 17:6; 19:15). Especially in a situation like that in Corinth, where Paul's word and ministry were being questioned, Paul needed to make clear that he was not simply making claims on his own, but making claims that his coworkers also would agree with.

This segment of 2 Corinthians is Paul's attempt to explain to his audience why he had not come as promised, as well as to explain a few other things. From a rhetorical point of view, this is part of a forensic discourse; it is important to focus

---

BIBLICAL BACKGROUND

"I" and "We" in 2 Corinthians and Elsewhere

As J. B. Lightfoot stresses, the letters written in Paul's name alone are Romans, Galatians, Ephesians, and the Pastoral Epistles. In all of these letters the singular is used by Paul, and the plural is *never* used to refer to himself alone. He uses the plural only where he is referring to himself as a member of a group (e.g., the apostles). This rule applies also to Philippians and Philemon, where we have the singular throughout (except Phil. 3:17, where there is a contextual reason). In 1 and 2 Thessalonians the plural is very seldom departed from, and note that these letters come from Paul, Silvanus, and Timothy.

> As a general rule we may say that wherever the communication is more directly personal then the singular is used, where it is more general the plural is preferred. . . . We may conclude: 1) that the plural "we" is not merely an epistolary "we" but it is connected with the plurality of persons in whose name the Epistle is written; 2) that so far from being correct to translate it "I" ordinarily, it is only to be so translated where the context shows that it clearly refers to the Apostle *alone*. 3) In every instance where the plural is used, we find that it will apply to those who are associated with the Apostle as well as the Apostle himself (except perhaps in 1 Thess 3:1, 2 where he distinctly states he is speaking of himself only—1 Thess 3:5).[a]

a. Lightfoot, *2 Corinthians*, 38–39.

on the relevant activities in the past that led to the accusation that Paul was just another slick salesman, in this case of the gospel, something that Paul will directly deny in his major thesis statement (2:17) immediately after this narration of unfortunate events.

What is presupposed is that Paul had indeed come to Corinth after writing 1 Corinthians, because that letter had not solved various problems, and Paul had been rebuffed and emotionally hurt by the experience. Apparently, he was severely criticized by one person in particular, as we shall see from this passage, and so he left quite wounded and deeply troubled about the Corinthian Christians. Because of the turmoil, Paul then had to write a "severe" or "sorrowful" letter to the congregation (which we do not now have), and fortunately, it seems to have largely had the desired effect, at least with most of the converts in Corinth.

So now, in 2 Corinthians Paul is writing a letter to comfort those stung by his rebuke, but also, as we shall see, to deal with some of the ongoing problems created by the pseudo-apostles who had impressed various Corinthians, which had led to some comparing Paul unfavorably to them. There is no reason to assume that these other missionaries were Peter or Apollos, both of whom Paul speaks positively about in 1 Corinthians. Early Christianity was not Jewish Christians pitted against Gentile Christians in general. After all, Paul and some of his converts were Jews, and some of Peter's converts certainly were Gentiles. But there were Pharisaic Jewish Christians who had caused trouble for Paul in Antioch and Galatia, and it is *not* apparent that those in Corinth are the same troublemakers. Notice that nothing is said in 2 Corinthians about circumcision, or Sabbath-keeping, or Jewish food laws (but see below on 2 Cor. 6:14–7:1).

In a narration of past events of this sort, events of relevance are the only ones mentioned, since they will help Paul later in this discourse defend his ministry and support his claims about how he relates to the Corinthians. Paul speaks first in verse 8 of some kind of severe trial in the province of Asia, which made Paul think that his death might be imminent. I agree with George Guthrie that had Paul been referring to Ephesus, he would have said so.[1] Asia was a major and large province in the west of what today is Türkiye, with Ephesus its capital.

The impression certainly is left that this fifty-something-year-old apostle would not rest until he was sure that his converts had changed their attitude about him and he could forgive them. So anxious was Paul about this that he decided not to pursue a very fruitful situation in Troas, a door that God had opened there to lead more to Christ, and instead crossed over into Macedonia, so perturbed was he that he had not found Titus in Troas as expected and so

---

1. See Guthrie, *2 Corinthians*, 79. He is right as well that the reference in 1 Cor. 15:32 to fighting with wild beasts in Ephesus should be taken to refer not to actual animals but rather to human opponents.

did not have his report of how things were going now in Corinth. Paul will continue his explanation for his perambulations at 2 Cor. 7:5, where his travels again become relevant to the discussion of the gospel issues he is raising.

The problem is in part that Paul does not appear to do what he promised, so here he must explain his change in itinerary, a change made to spare his audience, not to renege on a promise. Notice how Paul connects his own faithfulness to his word with the faithfulness of God in verses 17–22. He stresses that when God promises something, it is never yes and no but always yes. At the same time, being God's apostle, Paul himself strives to keep his word, even if it requires some midcourse corrections. The faithfulness of God should lead to the faithfulness of his apostle in regard to keeping promises.[2] Notice as well that Paul says that God's promises are fulfilled not in general but rather **in him**, in Christ. It is in Christ that **every one of God's promises is yes**, to which one can say, **"So be it, Amen."** God brings his plan, his promises, his prophecies to fulfillment in Christ. If one wants to know and understand God's plan for humanity, one must consider Christ and the work of Christ, including his death and resurrection. Too often people today try to understand God's prophecies and promises in light of one or another current event or circumstance, but Paul does not encourage us to do that. He encourages us to remember that God is fulfilling all promises not in history in general, or in disasters in particular, but in Jesus Christ.

The passing remark in 2:12 about passing up a ministry opportunity is telling for several reasons. God presented Paul with various possibilities, but it was up to Paul to assess and choose which was of greatest concern and urgency at the moment. This is very much like modern ministry when church leaders are presented with several good opportunities and choices and need to prayerfully and carefully make a decision. God does not always provide only one good path forward for ministry. But at the same time, sometimes leaders make decisions that are not according to God's will at that time, so sometimes God blocks what even a person like Paul thinks he should do. Paul wanted to go to Ephesus and do ministry in the province of Asia, but God, in the person of the Holy Spirit, had other things in mind for the apostle at that juncture (see Acts 16:6–10). Macedonia was to be approached first with the good news.

One of the major things one can learn from this passage, particularly in 2:5–11, is that it takes a mature Christian person like Paul not only to forgive a fellow believer who has wronged him but also then to encourage the Corinthians

---

2. Morna Hooker ("From God's Faithfulness to Ours") suggests that because Paul is in Christ, and God's faithfulness is embodied in the person of Christ and God's promises are only yes, and so reliable in Christ, therefore Paul himself could not be otherwise than faithful and reliable when it came to his words to the Corinthians about visiting and other matters. That is, what Paul is and also what he does are determined by the faithfulness of God.

to forgive that very person, and even to comfort them. Paul could have gone away and nursed his wounds and then tried to retaliate for the hurt done to him, but he did not. Rather, he followed the example of Christ and forgave his tormentor, whoever that was.

Paul speaks in the past tense of having been **anointed** (1:21), and not just him but also his coworkers. This involves a play on words, because the word for "anoint" is *chriō*, from which also comes *christos* ("Christ"). In essence, God has strengthened and christened us with Christ and also given us the Holy **Spirit in our hearts** (1:22). Notice the phrase **together with you** (1:21), which shows that these pregnant phrases apply not just to Paul and his coworkers but also to his audience. It is God the Father who has done this, so the entire Trinity is involved in our salvation.

A very major thing that we learn from this passage in 1:21–22 is about the Holy Spirit, whom Paul says God has placed in human hearts, our inner being. Thus, the living presence of God dwells within the believer. It is crucial to bear in mind that Paul affirms that the Holy Spirit is a person, not a mere force or power, and you don't get the Holy Spirit on the installment plan—some now, more later. I stress this because sometimes the reference to the Spirit being the *arrhabōn*, which one may translate as **down payment** or "deposit" (1:22), has led some to this sort of misunderstanding.

The living presence of the Spirit is a down payment on the rest of salvation, which will be delivered later—for example, at the return of Christ when the dead in Christ are raised. Paul is not talking about a first installment of the Spirit, as if one could get later installments in the future. He is talking about a first installment of salvation or everlasting life through the living presence of the Spirit in one's life. Furthermore, it is not entirely clear from the Greek text that the being **sealed** has anything to do with the **down payment**. In fact, three metaphors are used here—anointing, sealing, down payment—and they could all refer to different things. The Greek is clear enough that it is God the Father who has anointed us (and in this case the **us** seems clearly to be Paul and his coworkers, which is why he adds **with you** to **strengthens us**, where the **us** in that last phrase does not refer to the audience).

The additional *kai* ("also") in the Greek text at the beginning of verse 22 signals that the seal is something different from the anointing and strengthening. But what does it refer to? Revelation 7:3–8 suggests that it refers to a mark of ownership. Ephesians 1:13 and 4:30 mention being sealed with the promised Holy Spirit, and so possibly this phrase *does* go with the following one. In a business context a wax seal was used with scrolls to prevent them from being opened by the wrong person or at the wrong time. Whatever we make of this metaphor, it is clear that the word *arrhabōn* indicates that the giving of the

The Spirit—Not Just "May the Force Be with You"

Unfortunately, and in part because of some of the language used in the New Testament to describe the activity of the Holy Spirit (e.g., the Spirit is like the wind [John 3:5–8; Acts 2:1–4], or the talk of "being filled with the Spirit," as if one had some of the Spirit before but now one gets more of the Spirit), the Spirit at times has been treated as if the Spirit were an *it*, not a person. This is an enormous mistake. Paul warns against grieving the Spirit (Eph. 4:30), and we also can point to 1 Cor. 12:13, where the Spirit is said to be the person who baptizes a person into the body of Christ, and refer to the benediction in 2 Cor. 13:14, where the Father, Son, and Spirit are all said to be the source of blessing. In fact, as has long been emphasized by Gordon Fee in his classic study of the "Spirit" language in Paul's letters, Paul often predicates the very same things of Christ or the Father and the Spirit.[a] So, for example, the Spirit provides the fruit called "love" (Gal. 5:22), but elsewhere this same thing is said to come from God the Father or Christ.

Part of the reason for stressing the personal nature of the Spirit is that it is *as a person* that the Spirit indwells the believer, just as it is the person of Christ who indwells the believer (Col. 1:27). The believer isn't just empowered by some force called "spirit"; the believer is indwelled by the Spirit, who provides both fruit and gifts to believers. The language about being "filled with/by the Spirit" is Old Testament language that refers to a moment of inspiration or empowerment. *It does not refer to getting more of the Spirit than one had previously.* On the other hand, it is true that by progressive sanctification the indwelling Spirit can get hold of more aspects of the believer's inner self—renovating the mind, renewing the feelings, redirecting the will over the course of time—hence "progressive sanctification." Not surprisingly, the Holy Spirit is not just a giver of gifts or fruit, like some kind of divine Santa Claus; rather, the Spirit is a *Holy* Spirit, deeply concerned about the believer becoming more holy like the Father, Son, and Holy Spirit. Paul elsewhere emphasizes that the will of God for the believer is sanctification (1 Thess. 4:3), and the Spirit is the agent of that process (Rom. 15:16; 1 Cor. 6:11).

Jesus, in his Farewell Discourse (John 14–17), not only refers to the Holy Spirit as a person who convicts, convinces, and converts people (all of which are personal activities) but also calls him the *paraklētos*. Indeed, Jesus says that God the Father will send "another *paraklētos*" (John 14:16), with the implication that Jesus is the first one. In other words, Jesus himself indicates that the Spirit is a person like himself who will instruct God's people as he has done. While this word *paraklētos* is sometimes translated as "comforter," its basic meaning actually is "counselor" or "agent" or "legal advocate," and it refers to someone sent to convey some judgment or other kind of message; hence the Spirit is the one "who will lead you into all truth" (John 16:13).

a. Fee, *God's Empowering Presence*.

Spirit is crucial, but it's not the be-all and end-all of salvation; it is only the first installment, or down payment.[3] This language here of the deposit or down payment reflects Paul's use of business language, which we find elsewhere when he speaks about counting or reckoning, and about credits and debits (see, e.g., Rom. 4). It is not forensic or legal language.

Paul views salvation as coming in three stages: I *have been* saved (by grace through faith in Jesus), I *am being* saved (referring to the ongoing work of sanctification by the Spirit and the believers together working out their salvation as God works within the community to will and to do), and I *will be* saved (final salvation, when a person is fully conformed to the image of the risen Christ when he returns and raises the dead).

First Corinthians 12:13 had already made clear that "we were all baptized by the one Spirit so as to form one body, . . . and we were all given the one Spirit to drink." This makes clear that the Spirit is received at the point at which one is joined to the body of Christ, and he becomes an ongoing source of spiritual life from which the believer may draw. It is probably also good to make the point that Paul is talking about the baptizing action *by the Spirit*, not by the minister or some other human being. This being the case, he is not likely referring to water baptism, for in 1 Cor. 1:14 Paul says, "I thank God that I didn't [water] baptize more of you," because of the Corinthians making too much of the rite. I can't imagine Paul saying, "I thank God that more of you didn't receive baptism by the Holy Spirit."

In Rom. 6:1–14 Paul associates baptism with being baptized into Christ's death and thereby being buried with Christ, probably an image of the death of

---

3. Nothing is said here in 2 Corinthians about the Spirit sealing believers and making it impossible for them to commit apostasy or fall away. In any case, seals, whether on documents or jars, could be and were in fact meant to be broken at the appropriate time when they reached their intended recipient. It is unlikely that sealing is a metaphor for "once saved, always saved." Rather, as my former mentor Gordon Fee stresses, "For Paul, the gift of the Spirit is the first part of the redemption of the whole person, the beginning of the process that will end when believers assume their 'spiritual' bodies" (Fee, *God's Empowering Presence*, 294).

the old self (cf. below on 2 Cor. 5:17).[4] In all of this it is the Spirit who convicts, convinces, converts, and provides spiritual life to the believer in the form of gifts and fruit on an ongoing basis (Gal. 5:16–18, 22–26).

In his excellent study about holiness in the Pauline corpus, Ayodeji Adewuya rightly emphasizes the moral influence and capacities that the Spirit enables the believer to have, and he stresses the corporate nature in which Paul discusses such matters. "Paul always uses the word [*hagioi*, "holy ones" or "saints"] in [the] plural. He never uses the word to describe individuals. In other words, Paul's thinking on holiness is primarily communal, although each person who belongs to Jesus Christ belongs to him personally. There is nothing individualistic about this relationship. As such it is the church, collectively, that is called unto holy living, the individual only being important as a constituent member of the community."[5]

Adewuya rightly goes on to stress that various of the images that Paul uses to talk about the church collectively emphasize that they are to be morally pure, "chaste" (*hagnos*) in fact, as Paul himself has modeled as their moral exemplar (cf. 2 Cor. 6:6 and 11:2). The brief discussion in 2 Cor. 11:2 says that Paul has as a part of his mission to present the Corinthians as a pure or chaste "virgin" (*parthenos*) to Christ to be his bride. Interestingly, they are not yet viewed as the bride of Christ here, but as the betrothed.

Paul is undoubtedly drawing on the Old Testament image of Israel as betrothed to Yahweh (cf. Jer. 2:2, though usually the image is of Israel as already Yahweh's bride, as in Isa. 54:5–8). Another key image stressing holiness comes when Paul calls the Corinthians the "temple" (2 Cor. 6:16), in this case the *naos*, the holy of holies within the temple, the very place where God's living presence can be found, in this case within the Corinthian community. Again, as Adewuya stresses, it is the community, not individuals or subgroups, that is the locus of the indwelling Spirit.[6] He rightly goes on to stress that when talking about holiness, Paul is not just talking about some sort of spiritual experience, though that is involved; he is talking about behavior as well, such that the indwelling presence of the Spirit in the community should lead to "obedience in everything" (2 Cor. 10:6–7), but also to loving forgiveness of the individual who had sinned within the community but apparently repented (2:5–11). As 2 Cor. 6:1–10 makes apparent, Paul believes that reconciliation not only with God but also between himself and his contentious converts in Corinth should be the result of the Spirit's work in the Corinthian community. Drawing on Isa. 49:8 (LXX), Paul calls his converts to this reconciliation with God and their

---

4. On all this, see Witherington, *Troubled Waters*.
5. Adewuya, *Holiness in the Letters of Paul*, 65.
6. Adewuya, *Holiness in the Letters of Paul*, 69.

apostle. More could be said along these lines—for instance, in regard to 2 Cor. 6:14–7:1, where Paul calls for a radical break with the practice of going to pagan dinner parties at a pagan temple where other so-called gods are worshiped. Paul's monotheistic emphasis rules out compromise in these matters, not least because of the spiritual and moral pollution that one comes in contact with in such pagan dinner parties (see 1 Cor. 8–10). In Paul's view, this is a form of spiritual adultery because the Corinthians are already betrothed to the one true God, and are called to maintain spiritual and moral chastity as a result. It is well to bear in mind that "betrothal" in Paul's Jewish context was not like modern engagements, for betrothal was seen in early Judaism as the first act of marriage and part of a binding covenant or contract.

Near the end of this passage, at 2:11, Paul brings to the fore the person called the **Satan**, a word that comes from the Hebrew for "adversary." Paul certainly believes that this is a spiritual being having thoughts, intentions, plans to disrupt, divide, and if possible destroy Christian *koinōnia* and community. He is not merely referring to an evil force or power in the world. Notice as well that the behaviors of Paul and his converts are capable of thwarting Satan's **schemes**. Paul is aware of and wary of those thoughts or schemes (*noēma* literally means "thoughts," but in this case it refers to wicked thoughts and plans of Satan; cf. 3:14; 4:4; 11:3, where it refers to the thoughts in the minds of believers, negative thoughts that spiritually blind them).

Outside the Corinthian correspondence, Paul only rarely refers to Satan in one way or another (see, e.g., Rom. 16:20; Eph. 6:11 ["devil"]; 1 Thess. 2:18; 3:5 ["tempter"]), but in 1 and 2 Corinthians references are more common (1 Cor. 5:5; 7:5; 2 Cor. 2:11; 4:4; 6:15; 11:14; 12:7). Paul has an eschatological vision of the situation that he and his converts are in, and he believes that Christians have the resources to successfully oppose Satan's schemes and influences, because "greater is he who is in you" than these other spiritual influences in the world (see 1 John 4:4). In Eph. 6 Paul calls for his converts to *stand* and *withstand* the onslaught of temptation and abuse of the powers of darkness, and he believes that they can do so by faith and with the inner presence of the Spirit and the resources of the Word. Satan cannot make a Christian an offer they can't refuse, which is why he resorts to subterfuge, trying to bewitch, bother, and bewilder Christians and divide them.

This comports with what Paul says in 1 Cor. 10:13: "No temptation has overcome you that is not common to humanity such that with the temptation God provides an adequate means of escape." If Christ is the Lord of someone's life and the Spirit is indwelling, there is no room for other lordships in that person's life. In short, we should not be talking about Christians being demon-possessed, nor about Christians going on the offensive against Satan, whereas Eph. 6:10–17

"Do You Believe in Satan?"

I wasn't at all sure why my denomination had asked me to go see the conference counselor while I was in the ordination process to become an elder in the Western North Carolina Conference of the United Methodist Church (UMC), but it became apparent once I got to this counselor's office. When I sat down, he turned on a bank of cassette recorders (I don't remember being asked if I was okay with that), and then the questions started coming. I will explain why this might have happened. First, there was already a charismatic movement among United Methodists in the mid-1970s, as one form of the Good News movement, which sought to renew our church in a proper biblical way; and second, there was the fact that I was the first ordinand in that conference to choose to go to Gordon-Conwell Seminary in Massachusetts, an evangelical school endorsed by fellow Charlottean Billy Graham, instead of going to Duke or Candler, two nearby United Methodist seminaries. I guess they thought that I was some kind of fundamentalist, and they wanted to sound me out.

The first question was about Satan: "Do you believe in a personal being called Satan in the Bible?" My answer was yes. It seemed obvious to me not only from Scripture but also from experience that there was personal evil at work in the world. How better to explain the Holocaust, involving the murder of six million Jews, perpetrated by some of the most highly educated people in all of Europe, the Germans? My father, who fought in Germany in World War II, told tales of sheer wickedness on a massive scale that he witnessed when he helped liberate Germany from the Nazis.

I was then asked if I believed in demons as well. Again, my answer was yes. Jesus believed in them, and why shouldn't I, especially since there was contemporary evidence of demonic possession, and the Catholic Church even has a rite for an exorcism?

The next question was about speaking in tongues. Did I think that this was a valid spiritual gift for Christians today? Again, I answered in the affirmative. I felt that all my answers were the wrong ones. The end result of this process was that my ordination was delayed for a year, and I had to have my pastor at Myers Park UMC explain the issues to me. It was a wake-up call for me that there were consequences for believing what the Bible said about these matters rather than what some contemporary counselors and psychologists who worked for the UMC thought about them. Nevertheless, I was ordained a year later, when I came back from England after doing my PhD in the New Testament.

is about standing and successfully withstanding his assaults. In 2 Cor. 12:7 Paul refers to his thorn or stake in the flesh as a "messenger of Satan." Satan is seen as a person who can persecute and afflict even an apostle's body, but Paul never suggests that Satan can possess a Christian person.

An Inverted Triumph

One of the most interesting images that Paul conjures up in this discourse is at 2 Cor. 2:14–16, the notion that he is part of a triumphal procession, one led by Christ (cf. 1 Cor. 4:9). To really understand this passage, one needs to understand the nature of such Roman processions. During the Roman Republic, triumphant generals were regularly granted a triumphal procession in Rome, complete with floats, spoils of war, and captured prisoners, but by Paul's day only emperors were allowed to have such triumphs. This tells us something about how Paul views Christ: he is the reality of which the emperor is only a parody, and Christ's triumph transpires not through conquering and destroying other human beings, but by dying for them and then rising from the dead. It is interesting that even the emperor was reminded during the procession not to think too highly of himself, for there was a slave who would stand in the chariot with him and whisper, "*Memento mori*" (which can be translated, "Remember, you are mortal," or "Remember, you must die"), even though he wore red face powder, depicting him as the god of war, Mars or Mars in action, or some would say depicting him as Jupiter Optimus Maximus, the greatest of the gods in the pantheon of Roman deities.

Paul here depicts himself as a servant or slave of Christ with his same destiny (cf. 2 Cor. 4:10). Everyone knew that these processions led to the execution of the captives who had been enslaved, and Paul certainly believed that he had already been crucified with Christ (Gal. 2:19–20), and he could anticipate no different final literal outcome but a violent death for his service to Christ. This is why Paul speaks paradoxically of having the aroma of everlasting life for those embracing Christ, but also the stink of death to those who are dying. One would have to totally re-evaluate what counts as being triumphant and winning if a crucified and risen Jewish Messiah is the "Lord" who provides the example, and his suffering apostle is the more proximate model of how everlasting life and glory can be obtained—not by conquering others, but by winning them to Christ and surrendering to a Savior who provides atonement for all.

Finally, while Paul does refer to principalities and powers operating in the human sphere, he says next to nothing about demons, with the exception of 1 Cor. 10:20, where he refers to false gods as *daimonia*. It is important not to go beyond what the Scriptures actually say on these sorts of matters. The overall picture is that Paul is convinced that Christ and his people will win the battle against the powers of darkness, and that ultimately Satan's doom is sure, so he is working on borrowed time in the Christian era. In Rom. 16:19–20 Paul reassures his audience that if they will be wise as to what is good and avoid what is evil, then "God will soon crush Satan under [their] feet." Notice that it is God who is doing the crushing, *not* the believer. Notice as well that the Christian's deliberate focus on what is good and avoidance of evil paves the way for God to deal Satan a mighty blow so that he cannot harm or lead astray the believer. The probable reason why there are more references to Satan in the Corinthian correspondence than elsewhere in Paul's letters is that where there is major trouble in a group of house churches, Paul believes that the larger influence of Satan must be involved.

The Thesis of the Defense

> ^{2:17}**For we do not market for profit / peddle the Word of God, unlike so many. On the contrary, we speak with pure motives in Christ, speaking from God and before God.**

When one is forced to defend one's person, words and deeds, and authority, never mind one's ministry in general, there needs to be a basic proposition about what is and isn't true from Paul's point of view, and so in 2 Cor. 2:17 Paul states his case, and he contrasts himself and his actions with hucksters, slick salesmen, mere peddlers of God's Word, or "the truth." There was no lack of such hucksters in Paul's world. Consider, for example, what Lucian says about certain teachers of philosophy: "The philosophers sell their teaching like tavern-keepers, and most of them mix their wine with water and misrepresent it" (*Hermotimus* 59). Like in this critique, Paul refers to **so many** who behave that way. By contrast, Paul says, he speaks with pure motives, not to bilk someone of money, and he also says that he is **speaking from God and before God**.

It becomes clearer later in the letter that he is referring to his opponents in Corinth, the "super-apostles," a term used ironically, to say the least. Second Corinthians 1:12 provided a preview of what Paul would say here in the thesis statement, having already stressed his sincerity, honesty, and proper dealings with the Corinthians.[1] Let's be clear that Paul is not arrogantly contrasting himself with all other preachers of the gospel, including his own coworkers! He is,

---

1. Keener, *1–2 Corinthians*, 158–59.

however, aware of contrasting himself with many hucksters who are causing difficulties, including in Corinth.[2]

Lest we make the wrong sort of contrast here between Paul and these opponents, in both cases we are dealing with "pneumatics." Paul is perfectly clear in 1 Cor. 14 that he speaks in tongues quite a lot and, elsewhere in that same letter, that he speaks prophetically as well. Here he calls this **speaking from God**. But these "super-apostles" also claim to do similar things, even to the extent of bragging about being visionaries, which in turn prompts a reluctant Paul to talk about a time he once had a vision (2 Cor. 12:1–10).

If we miss the character of Paul's tongue-in-cheek boasting, and ironic and even sarcastic way of talking about his vision and other experiences, we will miss the fact that Paul is speaking the way he does in order to shame his audience into rejecting his opponents and their grandiose claims. The contrast here is not between those who have flashy spiritual gifts and those who don't, but rather between those who show off their gifts in an egocentric and self-promoting manner, even doing it to make money, and those like Paul, who don't exercise their spiritual gifts that way.

And here perhaps is a good place for a reminder that some of the most gifted persons in the body of Christ can also be some of the least spiritually mature. When God gives us gifts, it is up to us to decide how exactly we will use them: for our own glory and promotion, or for the glory of God. God's good gifts can be used or abused. Unfortunately, there is too often a lot of phony humility masking self-centered behavior. You can learn a lot about the character of someone's ministry by the fruit that it bears, or doesn't bear. And there are telltale signs in speech patterns as well.

When a person runs around talking about "my ministry" again and again, this is a dead giveaway that something is profoundly wrong. It's never "our ministry," which belongs to us; it's always the Lord's ministry working through us, and without the Lord we could accomplish nothing lasting, nothing of value. Of course, just as there is such a thing as false humility, so also there is such a thing as false pride. For example, no one should be proud of immoral behavior, whether the behavior involves how one spends one's money ("If you've got it, flaunt it"), or how one sexually behaves, or how one "rules" one's family with an iron hand, or how one tricks other people into buying something they do not need, or how one is skilled in bending the truth to get one's own way. And this is mostly overt behavior. There is also such a thing as hidden agendas.

As Paul stresses, he has no hidden agenda; he speaks from pure motives and with sincerity and transparency. He is being honest and forthright about why he

2. See the discussion in Thrall, *Second Epistle to the Corinthians*, 1:210–11.

felt it unwise to come back to Corinth at the time originally promised, among other things. And notice that the word **peddle** (*kapēleuontes* [here a participle]) has a rich history, previously used by Plato to refer to rhetorically verbose Sophists, those who loved to hear themselves talk and were "full of sound and fury but signifying nothing," striving just for mere eloquence (*Protagoras* 311b–e; cf. [Anaximenes of Lampsacus?], *Rhetoric to Alexander* pref. 1421a.32–34; Iamblichus, *Life of Pythagoras* 34.245). Paul uses the term in this very same way to critique the rhetoric of his opponents, who speak for profit or patronage.[3] The Corinthians were right to beware of rhetorical hucksters, which had been a problem for centuries. As Petronius reminds us, "When spongers are trying to get a dinner out of their rich friends, their main object is to find out what they would most like to hear. The only way they will get what they are after is by winning over their audience. It is the same with a tutor of rhetoric. Like a fisherman, he has to bait his hook with what he knows the little fish will rise for; otherwise, he is left on the rocks without a hope of their biting" (*Satyricon* 3).[4]

The phrase **from God and before God** is loaded. It refers to Paul preaching and writing not merely human words but God's inspired Word (see 1 Thess. 2:13), and it also conveys that he does so knowing that God is watching and evaluating. How his opponents evaluate Paul's speech and rhetoric is irrelevant. Paul is answerable to the one who called and equipped him—God.

If we ask why Paul's thesis statement alludes to people who speak for pay or profit, it is in part because Paul had refused patronage while in Corinth, and for a good reason: he did not want to become a client of some patron in Corinth. In 1 Cor. 9 Paul explained that although he had the right to be paid for his apostolic labors, he also had the right to turn down such pay, and he did so to avoid patronage and offer the gospel free of charge. But there was a second money issue in play as well. Paul had urged the Corinthians to set aside money for the collection for famine relief for the poor Jewish Christians in Jerusalem (1 Cor. 16:1–4; cf. Rom. 15:25–28). It is possible that Paul's refusal to take pay for his work, instead working with Priscilla and Aquila in his trade of leatherworking, led to suspicions that this was all a setup for his appeal to gather good sums of money for the collection. Whatever the case with that, Paul feels that he has to defend the collection at some length and encourage the Corinthians to participate (2 Cor. 8–9), as we shall see.

It needs to be noted, when we assess all of what Paul says about money and his own right to be paid (and note that in Philippians and elsewhere Paul is perfectly happy to participate in a relationship of "giving and receiving" with

---

3. See Kruse, *2 Corinthians*, 55.
4. Author's translation. See the helpful discussion in Garland, *2 Corinthians*, 152.

his converts, which is a parity relationship, not a patron-client relationship), that the modern notion that missionaries should adopt the "tentmaking" approach and thus pay their own way for work on the mission field is not soundly based in 1–2 Corinthians or elsewhere in the New Testament. That a worker is worthy of their hire is a principle that both Jesus and Paul affirmed. Paul is not here or elsewhere teaching that missionaries should *necessarily* be self-funded. There is no such gospel principle. Then as now, money has always been a delicate issue that can destroy the unity of a church, or of a ministerial staff, not to mention a whole denomination. Paul's relationship with the Corinthians was difficult compared to his relationship with the Philippians, and the latter paints the picture of a Paul perfectly willing to receive monetary support for his ministry. What Paul did not want, but what was on offer in Corinth, was "entangling alliances"—the inability to make clear that the gospel can be offered free of charge. But the Corinthians, like some moderns, seem to have had as their mantra, "You don't get something for nothing," or at least, "You get what you pay for." If it's something really valuable, then one should have to pay for it. Paul doesn't like or agree with such clichés. The good news and salvation are not for sale, but this does not mean that ministers shouldn't be paid, unless they decline the right to be so.

The Opening Argument, Part One

The Testimony of the Old Testament and the Corinthians

^{3:1}Are we beginning to commend ourselves again, or do we need letters of recommendation to you or from you, like some do? [No!] ²You yourselves are our letter, written on your hearts,[1] known and read by everyone. ³You show/reveal that you are Christ's letter, delivered by us, written not with ink on paper but with the Spirit of the living God, not on tablets of stone but on tablets of human hearts. ⁴Such is the confidence we have through Christ before God. ⁵Not that we are competent in ourselves to claim anything as if coming from ourselves, but our competency is from God, ⁶who has made us competent to be ministers of a new covenant, not of the letter but of the Spirit, for the letter kills, but the Spirit gives life.

⁷Now if the ministry of death, chiseled in letters on stones, came with glory so that the Israelites were not able to look intently at Moses's face because of its glory, [and] was transitory / brought to an end, ⁸how will the ministry of the Spirit not be more glorious? ⁹For if the ministry

---

1. Here some good manuscripts read "written on our hearts," and some "written on your hearts," but the latter makes much better sense in this context. Paul is appealing to the Corinthians themselves as exhibit A of the authenticity of his ministry. I have inserted into the translation "No!" in order to make clear that Paul is refuting the rhetorical question that begins the argument in verse 1.

that brought condemnation had glory, the ministry that brings righteousness exceeds with even more glory, [10]for that which had been glorious is not glorious now. [11]For if what was set aside was glorious, what endures will be even more glorious.

[12]Since, then, we have such a hope, we act with much boldness. [13]We are not like Moses, who used to put a veil over his face to prevent the Israelites from gazing steadily until the end of the glory of what was being set aside. [14]But their minds were hardened. For to this day, at the reading of the old covenant, the same veil remains. It is not lifted, because only in Christ is it set aside. [15]Still, even today, whenever Moses is read, a veil lies on their hearts, [16]but whenever a person turns to the Lord, the veil is removed. [17]Now the Lord [in this case] is the Spirit, and where the Spirit of the Lord is, there is freedom. [18]We all, with unveiled faces, are looking as in a mirror at the glory of the Lord and are being transformed into the same image, from glory to glory, which comes from the Lord, who is the Spirit.

In antiquity not all witnesses to the truth were considered of equal weight, and from a Jewish point of view the truth of anything needed to be confirmed by two or three different witnesses (cf. Deut. 17:6; 19:15). The strongest kind of witness was considered to be either official documents (in this case the Old Testament) or eyewitness testimony (in this case the Corinthians themselves). Such testimonies were considered to be strong because they were "inartificial," by which I mean that they were not made up out of the imagination or creativity of the defendant, being external to and independent of them. It is not an accident that Paul appeals to these kinds of unimpeachable witnesses to the authenticity of his ministry at the outset of his defense in 2 Cor. 3:1–18.

But what is the basis of Paul's competency in ministry? Interestingly, he insists that it is not these: (1) his long experience in serving God; (2) his education; (3) the various spiritual gifts he has; (4) his long endurance of suffering and his perseverance. No, Paul says that his competency is in God. Here he may be comparing himself to Moses, who claimed that he had a speech impediment or trouble speaking, to which God responded, "Who made the mouth but me?" (Exod. 4:10–12).

In short, it is God who makes the disabled able, who makes the inadequate adequate, who makes the unqualified qualified.[2] But ironically, Paul was one of the most qualified and well-educated, multilingual persons God could have chosen. What I suspect that Paul is primarily talking about is not the ability to

2. As aptly put by Guthrie, *2 Corinthians*, 195–96.

do the tasks assigned themselves but rather the competency and willingness to actually be an instrument in God's hands to change other people's lives. Plenty of people had skills, but God needed availability more than ability, willingness to suffer for the sake of the gospel, and, oddly enough, honesty and transparency about one's insufficiencies. But in a culture full of boasting, that sort of honesty could lead to critics questioning Paul's competency as a leader.

This is certainly one of the most complex arguments in all of Paul's letters, and it requires some careful unpacking in order to be understood. The first thing to notice is that Paul appeals to the genuine Christian experience of the Corinthians as proof positive that his ministry is authentic. This is the very same way he argues in Gal. 3, where he appeals to the experience of the Galatians (their hearing with faith is how they received the Spirit), then to the Old Testament example of Abraham, and then to custom or traditions or common sense. Here as well it is the converted Corinthians themselves who are seen as exhibit A that Paul is a genuine apostle of Christ. Then Paul turns to a fascinating discussion based in the experience of Moses and the Israelites at Mount Sinai as recorded in Exod. 34, which is seen as involving temporary glory compared to the enduring glory that Christ's followers see and have in him.

Let's be clear that what we have here is a tale of two covenants, the Mosaic one and the new one. And this is the very first time in any ancient document that the Mosaic covenant is called **the old covenant**. The contrast here is not between Word and Spirit, or law and Spirit, nor is it between literal interpretations of God's words and pneumatic ones (despite Origen and others thinking that it is);[3] rather, it is between the *effect* of the old covenant on fallen and sinful human beings and the *effect* of the new covenant. Further, this is not a lauding of the Spirit at the expense of God's Word. Elsewhere Paul is perfectly clear that the law of Moses is holy and good (see, e.g., Rom. 7:12), and that commandments are good and from God. The problem is that the *effect* of the law on fallen persons is condemnation, not redemption, whereas the *effect* of the message of the new covenant, administered by the Spirit, is rejuvenation: we become new creatures in Christ. The law can tell a person what they ought to do and be, but it cannot enable them to do it and be it, since all have sinned and fallen short of God's glory. Furthermore, it was God who inscribed the letters on stone for Moses, just as the Spirit inscribes the law on human hearts. So, we must not make the mistake of too radically contrasting **letter** and **Spirit** in this passage.

---

3. See Witherington, *Sola Scriptura*.

There is, of course, only one significant reference to a new covenant in the Old Testament, and it is found in Jer. 31:31–34, which reads,

> "The days are coming," declares the LORD,
>   "when I will make a new covenant
> with the people of Israel
>   and with the people of Judah.
> It will not be like the covenant
>   I made with their ancestors
> when I took them by the hand
>   to lead them out of Egypt,
> because they broke my covenant. . . .
> This is the covenant I will make with the people of Israel
>   after that time," declares the LORD.
> "I will put my law in their minds
>   and write it on their hearts.
> I will be their God,
>   and they will be my people.
> No longer will they teach their neighbor,
>   or say to one another, 'Know the LORD,'
> because they will all know me,
>   from the least of them to the greatest,"
>
>   declares the LORD.
> "For I will forgive their wickedness
>   and will remember their sins no more." (NIV)

This calls for a brief look at this text in more detail (see the sidebar "The New Covenant").

It is hard to follow the logic of Paul's argument here unless one is looking at the text of Exod. 34 as well as 2 Cor. 3. In the story in Exod. 34, **Moses** has to wear a **veil** when he is speaking to the people because the **glory** on his face bothers or is threatening to God's sinful people, who have been busy making a golden calf. But when Moses turns to where the Lord's presence is to be found, in this case in the tabernacle, he can remove the veil. Similarly, Paul is saying to the Corinthians that when someone repents and turns to the Lord, the **veil** over their heart, and their inability to understand God's Word, **is removed**. As N. T. Wright puts it, "The Lord in this text [Exod. 34] can be seen as a reference to the Spirit, the sovereign one who softens hearts and changes lives, who brings new life in the present and guarantees for the future (1:21–22)."[4] This is exactly right. Paul is not confusing or fusing the risen Lord Christ with the Holy Spirit;

---

4. Wright, *Paul for Everyone: 2 Corinthians*, 38.

rather, he is saying that "Lord" in the Exodus text refers to the Spirit of God because the Spirit is the change agent.

The comparison of the Mosaic covenant with the new covenant is not intended to be a straight contrast, but rather a "how much more" comparison between two good things. This is a well-known rhetorical device called *synkrisis*, which sometimes takes the form of comparison of somewhat alike things or persons, but mostly involves a contrast (see, e.g., the contrast between Adam

BIBLICAL BACKGROUND

The New Covenant

There was debate in early Judaism concerning whether Jeremiah was talking about either a renewed or a genuinely new covenant, but the evidence favors the idea that this is not about renewal of the Mosaic covenant. First, as Deborah Endean has shown, the linguistic evidence favors the interpretation that something genuinely new is meant.[a] Second, there is a clear contrast in Jer. 31 between the covenant made with the ancestors, which surely refers to the Mosaic covenant and perhaps also the Abrahamic covenant, and the new covenant written on human hearts, which is why the text goes on to say that God's people will not need to be told, "Know the LORD"; they will all know God because of this internal inscribing of the covenant. Third, notice that the contrast is not between a law covenant like the Mosaic covenant and the new covenant. Indeed, it is said that the new covenant involves *law*, albeit law written on human hearts. This explains why Paul, who is drawing on Jer. 31 in 2 Cor. 3, will elsewhere talk about the law of Christ. The new covenant is not a law-free or commandment-free covenant, and obedience to those commandments is not optional. Fourth, Jeremiah says that this new covenant is for the people of Israel and Judah (i.e., the northern and southern tribes). This is not surprising, and it may partially explain why Paul stresses in Rom. 1 that even the gospel about the Messiah and the new covenant is for the Jew *first*, and also the Gentile. In order for Gentiles to take part in the new covenant, they will have to receive the gospel from its Jewish proclaimers and form a community of Jew and Gentile united in the new covenant and in Christ.

a. Endean, "Theological and Exegetical Study of *ḥādāš*." This is her doctoral thesis, done on the use of the "new" language in the Hebrew Bible, including in Jeremiah and Isaiah. The dissertation was done at Asbury Theological Seminary and successfully defended in 2021.

Anubis, the deity with the black jackal-shaped head, was the god who helped the deceased get into the positive afterlife. The heart of the person in question is in a vessel on the scale on the left side, whereas on the scale on the right side is a feather, an emblem of truth. So, the judgment scene depicts a person's heart being weighed for its truthfulness.

and Christ in Rom. 5:12–21) or, as here, a comparison between two good things, though the element of contrast (temporary versus permanent covenant, fading versus everlasting glory) is not absent. If the Mosaic covenant involved Word and Spirit and glory, the shining presence of God in a life, *how much more* does the new covenant involve these things, and not on a temporary basis that fades away, but forever. The Spirit illuminates the minds of Paul's converts about God's Word when they turn to the Lord, and the veil or hard-heartedness is removed. Further, the Spirit enables obedience to God's Word, as the Spirit sets the believer free from the ruling principle and bondage of sin and death (Rom. 8:1–4).

It helps to have Ezek. 11:19 and 36:26 in mind as well when studying 2 Cor. 3, Old Testament texts that refer to the removal of a heart of stone and its replacement with a heart of flesh by means of putting a new spirit within a person. Paul is drawing on both of these prophetic sources in this part of his discourse. He is implying that these Scriptures have been fulfilled through his own ministry with the Corinthians, for they received the Spirit and have been changed by the gospel.[5] The Israelites had suffered too long from hardening of the spiritual arteries, and Ezekiel prophesies that a day will come when this problem will be remedied by the Spirit of God.

Notice that both Jer. 31 and also various places in 2 Corinthians before the final major argument in 2 Cor. 10–13 (cf. 1:22; 2:4; 3:2–3, 15; 4:6; 5:12; 6:11; 7:3; 8:16; 9:7) talk about the *kardia*, the "heart." In various ancient Near Eastern

5. See Garland, *2 Corinthians*, 160–61.

cultures, for instance in Egypt, the heart was seen as the control center of the person—the center of thought, feeling, and will. In hieroglyphic wall paintings we see again and again a human heart being weighed in scales, when a deceased person faces the final judgment on the quality of his or her life.

The psalmist urges God to search and know his heart, to test and know his anxious thoughts (Ps. 139:23–24). In 2 Corinthians, not only does Paul use the term "heart" in this way, but also he stresses that the heart is the place the Spirit dwells and works (1:22; 3:3), and so not surprisingly it is the place where enlightenment takes place (3:15; 4:6). But Paul can also use the term "heart" in a different metaphorical way to refer to a person's commitment or even integrity (5:12; 6:11; 8:16; 9:7).[6]

This passage will make a good deal more sense as the discourse goes on, but here Paul is making clear that he has spoken honestly, not deceptively; plainly, not with large rhetorical flourishes; and boldly, not timidly, risking possible personal rejection by some in his audience. The word *parrhēsia* refers literally to speaking freely and frankly in 3:12. His was not a ministry of currying favor with his audience in order to become popular, or get paid, unlike the "super-apostles." And this brings up a vital point for us today. All too often it is easy for a minister who is being paid for his or her ministry to gradually turn into a people-pleaser rather than a God-pleaser, because psychologically there is that little voice in one's head that says, "I'm dependent on these people for my livelihood, so I need to be nice and not offend them." Whatever else one could say about Paul, he was not a mere people-pleaser, and again and again it cost him to tell the unvarnished truth not only about God but about the sins of his audience. Indeed, it led to persecution and suffering at numerous points. Jesus did not say, "Take up your salary and retirement account and follow me"; he said, "Take up your cross and follow me," and Paul took that absolutely seriously.

6. Here I am following the helpful discussion by Guthrie, *2 Corinthians*, 188.

The Opening Argument, Part Two

Eternal Treasures in Earthen Vessels

⁴:¹Therefore, since we have this ministry, insofar as we were shown mercy, we do not give up, ²but have renounced the secret and shameful things, not acting deceitfully or distorting the Word of God but, through an open display of the truth, commending ourselves to everyone's conscience, before God. ³But if our gospel is veiled, it is veiled to those who are perishing; ⁴in them the god of this age has blinded the mind of these unbelievers, to keep them from seeing the light of the gospel about the glory of Christ, who is the image of God. ⁵For we are not proclaiming ourselves, but Jesus Christ as Lord, and ourselves as your servants on account of Jesus. ⁶For God, who said, "Out of darkness let light shine," has shone in our hearts to give the light of the knowledge of the glory of God in the face of Christ.

⁷But we have this treasure in clay vessels in order that the extraordinary quality of the power of God may be [seen to be] from God and not from us. ⁸We are afflicted in every way but not crushed, perplexed but not in despair, ⁹persecuted but not abandoned, struck down but not destroyed, ¹⁰always carrying around the death of Jesus in the body, so that the life of Jesus may also be displayed in our body. ¹¹For we the living are always being given over to death for Jesus' sake, so that Jesus' life may be displayed in our mortal flesh. ¹²So then, death is at work in us, but life in you. ¹³But having the same spirit of faith according to what is

written—"I believed, therefore I spoke"—we also believe and therefore speak.

[14]For we know that the one who raised the Lord Jesus will also raise us with Jesus and present us with you. [15]For everything is because of you in order that the grace may extend through the many, so it may cause thanksgiving to increase to the glory of God. [16]Therefore we do not lose heart. Even though outwardly we are being destroyed, inwardly we are being renewed day by day, [17]for the lightness of our momentary afflictions is producing for us out of all proportion an incomparable weight of glory for us. [18]So we are not focusing on what is seen, but rather on what is unseen. For what is seen is temporary, but what is unseen is eternal. [5:1]For we know that if our earthly tent in which we live is destroyed, we have a building from God, an eternal house in the heavens not made with hands. [2]For we even groan in this tent, desiring to put on our heavenly dwelling, [3]since when we have taken the tent off, we will not be found naked. [4]Indeed, we groan while in this tent, being burdened, because we don't want to be unclothed but be further clothed, so that mortality may be swallowed up by life. [5]But the one who has prepared us for this very purpose is God, who gave us the Spirit as a down payment. [6]Therefore we are always confident and know that as long as we are at home in the body we are away from the Lord. [7]For we walk according to faith, not by sight. [8]But being confident, we would rather be away from the body and at home with the Lord. [9]Therefore, whether we are at home or away, we make it our aim to be pleasing to him, [10]for we must all appear before the judgment seat of Christ, so that each may be repaid for what we have done in the body, whether good or evil.

Paul's vivid descriptions in this part of the discourse have caused no little confusion and have even led some scholars to think that Paul changed his eschatology, his end-times thinking, between the writing of 1 Corinthians and the writing of 2 Corinthians, moving from a classic Pharisaic belief about bodily resurrection at the return of Christ (1 Cor. 15) to a theology of dying and going to heaven. That would indeed be a Copernican revolution of a change in his thinking, but it's entirely unlikely, especially since these two letters were written only a short time apart, maybe two or so years. What is true, as we shall see, is that after all the physical abuse of Paul, not to mention all the mental trauma, Paul does reflect in 2 Cor. 4:1–5:10 about dying and going to heaven, leaving behind the earthly body, which he here aptly calls a **tent**—a temporary and rather flimsy dwelling that a tentmaker such as Paul would naturally use as an analogy.

To be completely clear, Paul in this passage conceives of three states: (1) dwelling on earth in our present, temporary body (called a **tent**); (2) dwelling in heaven with the Lord without the present temporary physical body, with the heavenly dwelling *place* being called a **building . . . not made with** [human] **hands** (cf. Acts 7:48–50 for Stephen's use of the phrase); and (3) being further clothed with a resurrection body, which is immune to suffering, sin, and sorrow, immune to disease, decay, and death. Paul sees this last condition much to be preferred to the interim condition of being absent from the body and present with the Lord, though that is clearly better than his present suffering. One last bit of introduction: Paul, like other early Jews, did not believe in the Greco-Roman idea of the immortal soul. Rather, he believed in the human spirit, which involved all the nonmaterial parts of one's personhood and personality, going to be with God. This is also what we hear about from Jesus on the cross when he says, "Father, into your hands I commit my spirit" (Luke 23:46). Bearing these things in mind, we can now walk through this passage and understand it better.

Paul begins this part of the argument by saying that he is not discouraged or losing heart, because by God's mercy the ministry continues to bear good fruit. Paul makes clear that he does not follow the practices of unethical orators or teachers. He doesn't use cunning or deceit; rather he speaks with transparency, the plain unvarnished truth of the gospel. His conscience is clear about this, and he commends that conscience to everyone, in the sight of God.

All along in this discourse Paul is preparing for a more direct critique of his opponents who are currently bewitching some Corinthians. He is slowly drawing up a character sketch of what they are actually like and what they are doing to the Corinthians. And the character sketch perfectly describes the Sophist, the rhetorician who is in it for attention, personal gain, even to the point of being willing to distort or bend the truth. Philo, a contemporary of Paul, describes such people as follows: "Imposters, flatterers, inventors of cunning plausibilities, who know well how to cheat and mislead, but that only, and have no thought for honest truth" (*Who Is the Heir?* 302).[1] By contrast, Paul depicts himself as someone who uses *parrhēsia*, literally, "free speech," which is the opposite of subterfuge or deception. And as we shall see, this has something to do with the orator's appearance and the way he speaks, which Paul's critics contrast with his letters.

Now, just because Paul's message is clear and straightforward doesn't mean that everyone will obviously get the point or embrace it. Why not? Because, says Paul, **the god of this** current evil **age** (2 Cor. 4:4; cf. Gal. 1:4) **has blinded the minds of unbelievers**. This is clearly enough a reference to Satan, not God

1. See the discussion in Garland, *2 Corinthians*, 206n500.

Let Your Conscience Be Your Guide?

In 2 Cor. 4:2 Paul uses the word *syneidēsis*. He one is of the very few writers in the New Testament who talks about *syneidēsis*, a word properly translated as "conscience," though its basic meaning is "consciousness," and it came to have the sense of moral consciousness. Unlike much of the modern use of the word "conscience," Paul uses the term to refer to a moral faculty that can either approve or disapprove of some potential or actual decision or action. It does not refer to merely negative moral judgments or warnings. In any case, Paul would not have advised, "Let your conscience be your guide," because one needs an external check and balance—namely, the Word of God—and because, as he will say shortly, the human conscience of unbelievers is corrupted, blinded by "the god of this age" (4:4).

Nevertheless, Paul believes that some good effect can come from an appeal to the conscience of anyone, since while their conscience may be darkened by sin, it has not been eliminated altogether, and God's light can penetrate that darkness. Karl Barth once famously suggested that sometimes resorting to apologetics and mere reason appealing to conscience will not work with an unbeliever; rather, one has to hurl the gospel at them like a stone through a plate-glass window, shattering their complacency, their worldview, their defenses. Paul is not doing that to the Corinthians in this discourse, but you can see how he takes on the "super-apostles," pulling out all the stops to expose them for what they are: imposters, peddlers, Sophists.

(see 2 Cor. 6:14–25 and Phil. 3:19).[2] This is the only place in the New Testament where Satan is called "god," and the point is that he is powerful and at work to prevent unbelievers from seeing and understanding the gospel. Just because they can't mentally see, understand, or accept it doesn't mean that it isn't true, any more than the fact that a blind person can't see the sun doesn't mean that there isn't one.[3]

Paul has a clear and robust understanding of viable secondary causes, by which I mean he does not believe that God is the cause directly or indirectly of evil. There are other forces besides God in the world that have some power and

2. See Keener, *1–2 Corinthians*, 173.
3. An analogy made by Hodge, *Second Epistle to the Corinthians*, 84.

agency, including the devil, angels, and human beings as well. The sovereign God has made this possible, so even though there is no equal to the real God in this world, being the only all-powerful and all-knowing being, there are others who can act, even act against and violate the will of God. This is why Paul, when he assures Christians about how things will turn out, says things like, "God can work all things together for good for those who love him" (Rom. 8:28). Notice that Rom. 8:28 does not say that everything that happens is good in itself, but rather that God can work all things together for good.

Sadly, however, some early Christian theologians overreacted to the misuse of this passage (**the god of this age has blinded . . .**) by Marcion, who used this phrase to justify his view that the God of the Old Testament is not the same God revealed in Jesus Christ. Tertullian made this mistake by failing to realize that Paul is not talking about any proper deity—Father, Son, or Holy Spirit—but about Satan. And worse still, the Arians used this verse to say that since Satan can be called a god, the fact that Christ is called this is no proof of his divinity! This led to the overreaction by no less than John Chrysostom, Hilary, and even Augustine.[4] In the case of Augustine, the problem was that he himself had a defective view of how God exercised his sovereignty, which is to say, he had no viable understanding of actual secondary causes, such as the actions of Satan being independent of and in fact against God's will.

Perhaps the most frequent term Paul uses for non-Christians in 1–2 Corinthians is "unbelievers" (1 Cor. 6:6; 7:12–15; 10:27; 14:22–24; 2 Cor. 4:4; 6:14–15; see also 1 Tim. 5:8; Titus 1:15). The term is not intended to pass judgment on the eternal destiny of such people, since Paul's letters and the book of Acts are replete with stories of unbelievers becoming believers by the grace of God, and by embracing the salvation that Christ offers by faith. Rather, for Paul, it is simply a statement of fact, a statement about the sad state of this present evil age, in which Satan is at work trying to prevent unbelievers from becoming believers. There is another force at work in this dark age—namely, God—and Paul reassures his Roman audience, "The God of peace will soon crush Satan under *your* feet" (Rom. 16:20). This is probably not about some eschatological or final judgment on the devil, but rather about how God is actively working against Satan's influence in the Christian community. This comports with Paul's confidence even in 2 Corinthians that things will ultimately turn out well in Corinth, because God is at work among the Christians there.

In 2 Cor. 4:4 Paul calls Christ **the image of God** (cf. Col. 1:15; see also John 14:9), something previously said about God's Wisdom, as depicted in Prov. 2:4; 3:8–9 and in the Wisdom of Solomon, especially Wisd. 7:14, 26. Christ is, then,

---

4. See the discussion in Garland, *2 Corinthians*, 210, and the notes.

The Image of God

In 2 Cor. 4 we hear about Christ being the mirror image of God the Father, which leads us to phrases by the Johannine Jesus such as, "Anyone who has seen me has seen the Father" (John 14:9). The idea as applied to Christ is that he shares the same character and nature as the Father and is fulfilling the will and salvation plan of the Father. They are both part of the divine identity. Here Paul is not talking about the more general idea that human beings are created in the image of God, which in Gen. 1 is coupled with the notion of "likeness." The text says, "Let us make humankind in our image and after our likeness" (Gen. 1:26). Scholars have debated whether this is simply two ways to talk about the same thing, and they have debated endlessly in what way humans are said to be "like" God (does it have to do with our ability to create other human beings, or fill the earth and subdue it, being cocreators and corulers with God of the earth?). Possibly of relevance is that the Hebrew word *tselem*, translated as "image," is in fact the same word used to refer to an "idol." Now, the function of an idol in the ancient Near East was to represent the deity in question in a particular place and to be a sort of conduit of that deity's power and presence. Was the writer of Gen. 1 thinking of human beings as conveyors of the divine presence and power, while at the same time not making humans into divine beings? These are some of the issues the text of Gen. 1 raises, and also Ps. 8, which suggests humans in the creation order are above all other earthly creatures and but a little lower than the angels (8:4–8). But this is not the message that Heb. 1:1–14 wants to convey about Christ. There we learn that Christ, or at least the now-exalted Christ, is (1) not to be identified as or with angels (he is not, for instance, the angel of the Lord in the Old Testament) but (2) far above them in the order of sentient beings. We also hear that Christ was a cocreator of the universe with the Father (again drawing on what is said about personified Wisdom in Prov. 3; 8), and Heb. 1:3 says Christ is the radiance and very imprint of the Father, and here an indebtedness to the discussion of Wisdom in Wisd. 7:26 seems clear. Here Christ is not merely a reflection of the Father but rather a manifestation of the divine identity of God the Father. One of the things that changes when one reads all of the "image" language used by Paul, and in this case of believers, is that he prefers to talk about believers being transformed into the likeness of Christ (see, e.g., 2 Cor. 3:18). This may be connected to his discussions about (1) the need for us to imitate Christ as Paul himself does (1 Cor. 11:1) and (2) the fact that in the end believers will be fully conformed to the image of Christ by obtaining a resurrection body when Christ returns (see 1 Cor. 15; cf. Rom. 8:28–30).[a]

a. See Witherington, *Jesus the Sage;* Witherington, *Letters and Homilies for Jewish Christians,* 100–106.

the fulfillment of this idea that previously was just a personification of God's mind or wisdom. The gospel of the glory of Christ is said to be light—something that reveals the truth, the real situation in the world, one's personal situation, one's need for redemption.

Second Corinthians 4:5–6 summarizes the gospel that Paul preaches, and the one he doesn't preach. He preaches **Christ** as the risen **Lord**, and himself and his coworkers as Christ's **servants**, but also servants of the Corinthians. Paul does not preach himself. Certainly, one of the earliest and most fundamental Christian confessions is that Jesus Christ is the risen Lord (see Rom. 10:9; 1 Cor. 12:3). At the very heart of the earliest professions of faith is Christ crucified and risen, and God having made him Son of God in power, or Lord of all by means of the resurrection (see Rom. 1:3–4; Phil. 2:5–11). During his earthly ministry Jesus was Son of God in weakness, and he preferred to call himself the Son of Man, alluding to Dan. 7:13–14, the only Old Testament text that mentions the two phrases or ideas most constantly on Jesus' lips: "Son of Man" and "kingdom of God."

All this raises the question of whether and how much Christology actually gets preached in the modern church, even in charismatic or Pentecostal or Wesleyan contexts (see the sidebar "What Then Shall We Preach?").

As Frank Matera points out, the verses of 2 Cor. 4:10–12 are important because they

> indicate that Paul views the apostolic hardships listed in vss. 8–9 in terms of Christ's death and resurrection, or as he writes, "the dying of Jesus" and "the life of Jesus." His sufferings are more than personal afflictions; they are a participation in the death and rising of Jesus. Despite them, or more accurately, *because of them*, the life of Jesus is manifested in Paul's body . . . , which he equates with his mortal flesh. . . . The result of this process is that Paul's hardships effect "life" in the Corinthians, recalling what he said in the opening benediction, "If we are afflicted, it is for your consolation and salvation" (1:6).[5]

Paul then turns in 2 Cor. 4:13 to Ps. 116, quoting one verse in it. But the entire psalm is relevant to Paul's own situation, as it refers to God rescuing someone from the pangs of death, from a near-death experience, from people lying about that person, even though he had faith in God and spoke faithfully. The whole tone of the psalm is one of gratitude for God's mercy, and this is also where Paul finds himself as he is writing this discourse.[6]

5. Matera, *II Corinthians*, 110.
6. See Wright, *Paul for Everyone: 2 Corinthians*, 47–49.

In 4:16–17 Paul presents us with an image of scales in which we learn what has more weight, more value. In one pan of the scales there are things that are temporal and temporary: suffering, sorrow, sickness, disease, decay, and death, with the outward body wasting away. But in the other pan of the scales there is the eternal **weight of glory**, there is everlasting life. The afflictions suffered now are not light in themselves, but rather in comparison to what is in the other pan in the scales: the eternal weight of glory.

As this argument moves along, it becomes clear that Paul is not ultimately a dualist, by which I mean a person who sees the body as bad, even the prison house of the soul, and the inner self or spirit of a person as good. As a Pharisaic Jew, he sees the body as ultimately an essential part of the human identity, so much so that God has plans to reunite his people with permanent bodies, resurrection bodies. It is not an accident that the historic burial liturgy used for many centuries has the minister say at the grave, "Ashes to ashes, dust to dust, in sure and certain hope of the resurrection." Notice that it does not say "in sure and certain hope of dying and going to heaven," though that is affirmed as well.

The problem is that since the church has been going for almost two thousand years now, the afterlife theology about the resurrection and the eschatological future on earth, which makes up more than 90 percent of the discussion of the afterlife in the New Testament, has been displaced by the minor theme of dying and going to heaven, which is not viewed as the Christian's final destiny in the New Testament. Rather, it is seen as a good interim state on the way to the resurrection and the kingdom of God on earth, as it is in heaven.

But what in the world does Paul mean when he says **we have a building from God, an eternal house in the heavens not made with hands**? (2 Cor. 5:21). While some have assumed that this is a reference to there being resurrection bodies in heaven in a sort of heavenly freezer locker waiting for us, this is unlikely.[7] The resurrection body comes from the earth or from transformation on the earth (see 1 Cor. 15; 1 Thess. 4). It is more likely to me that this is a reference to what Paul elsewhere calls "the Jerusalem that is from above" (Gal. 4:26), or even the heavenly "Zion" (Rom. 11:26). After all, in Acts 7:48 Stephen speaks of a house not made with human hands, in reference to God's house in heaven. And note that in John 14:2 Jesus says, "In my Father's house there are many rooms." Further, the author of Hebrews talks readily about the heavenly sanctuary (Heb. 8:5; 9:24). So, I would interpret **a building from God, an eternal house in the heavens** as referring not to individual human resurrection bodies but rather to the heavenly house with many rooms, which Jesus has prepared for the believers.

7. See, e.g., Matera, *II Corinthians*, 113–22.

What Then Shall We Preach?

Any close reader of the Corinthian correspondence will realize that for Paul, Christ and him crucified and risen, Christ as the risen Lord, Christ as the savior, redeemer of the lost, and the object and basis of faith is perhaps the most fundamental thing any Christian preacher can preach. But how often do we hear such sermons in the church these days? Not very often, I'm afraid. Yes, occasionally, we hear this if we have an evangelistic service or two, or at Easter, when one can hardly avoid saying something about the cross and the resurrection, or perhaps at a revival meeting. But what most often happens especially in low-church Protestant services is (1) a sermon series on topics of recent importance; or (2) an interview or dialogue with other pastors or teachers about the current crisis in the church; or (3) a testimony by some missionary or evangelist, or even a local person, about what God is doing, or how some besetting sin has been overcome, and so forth. What we do not get is detailed preaching on the person and work of Christ himself, or Christ and the doctrine of salvation.

We need to remind ourselves: what we have in Paul's letters is not evangelism. We can look at the sermon summaries in Acts for those sorts of sermons. No, Paul's letters *are addressed to Christians, albeit Christians with problems, and yet on almost every page Paul is presenting some aspect of Christology or pneumatology or Patrology (the doctrine of the Father) that is relevant to the audience's dealing with both theological and ethical problems.*

Paul's preaching is not about himself and his accomplishments. Paul is not taking a poll on what subjects the Corinthians would like to know more about. No, he is preaching and teaching the heart of the gospel itself, which is eternally relevant and needed. Paul does not take a consumer approach to his discourse. He offers what the congregation *needs* to hear, not necessarily at all what they *would like* to hear. He is not like preachers who preach to the desires and wants of the congregation. He preaches what God desires and requires.

If we ask why modern preachers in low-church Protestant churches are not following the example of Paul's christologically and spiritually rich preaching, there are a few reasons we can mention: (1) a near total lack of actual deep study of the Scriptures in their original contexts by such preachers, and basically no study of the Scriptures in Greek or Hebrew; (2) a lack of reading of good detailed commentaries that are not simply addressing the current situation or the problems of our current culture, but rather are grounding us in God's Word and in Christ in a profound way; (3) a failure to make the needed time and effort to do (1) and (2) properly.

The end result is a superficial use of Scripture that does not lead people into a deeper walk with Christ, a deeper knowledge of the Word, or a more profound commitment to the confessions of our faith that have existed ever since the time of Jesus and Paul. Perhaps it is time for us to stop insulting the intelligence of our congregations, stop dumbing down the gospel, stop putting the cookies on the bottom shelf and instead to start challenging our people with the meat of the gospel, teasing their minds into active thought. But this requires that preachers themselves be regularly and profoundly grounded in God's Word. Perhaps it is time for all ministers to rededicate themselves to lifelong learning of God's Word and how to preach significant portions of Scripture, not little sound bites from here, there, and yonder in the Bible. It was Chaucer who said, "If gold rusts, what then will iron do?" He was referring to what happens when a minister fails to set a Christlike example and preach the genuine gospel. Unless ministers set the proper example, they cannot expect the people of the congregation to become all they ought to be.

As has rightly been stressed by various commentators, Paul knows of three states: (1) life in this temporary tent (body) here and now, (2) life in heaven, which involves being **away from the body and at home with the Lord** (5:8), which Paul can also refer to as nakedness, a condition he would rather avoid (if the choice is between living on earth until the further clothing with a resurrection body or dying and being without a body) because he would rather have (3) life further clothed with the resurrection through transformation of his present body. Clothed, **unclothed**, **further clothed**—these are the three possible conditions, for the believers in heaven do not have bodies; they are spirits in the presence of God.[8]

Finally, there are two small but significant points against taking **we have a building . . .** to indicate individual resurrection bodies in heaven: (1) the **we** is talking about something collectively shared by believers in heaven; (2) **building** in the Greek is in the singular (accusative singular feminine noun), so it is not "we have buildings in heaven." And of course, Paul is mixing his metaphors,

8. As Margaret Thrall points out, had Paul meant "absent from this body," we would expect *ek tou sōmatos toutou*, but that's not what he says. He says "absent from *the* body" (Thrall, *Second Epistle to the Corinthians*, 1:391).

since buildings are not clothing that can be put on, never mind put on over the existing clothing. What Paul is striving to say is that he would rather not be naked in the presence of God in heaven, but would rather be further clothed with a resurrection body while still alive on earth in this present tent. However, there is the consolation that when one goes to heaven, absent from the body but at home with the Lord, one shares Christ's home with him—the heavenly Zion or new Jerusalem.

Some commentators have suggested that the resurrection body is assumed at death and is a spiritual body, but this makes little sense of a text like 1 Thess. 4:13–17, where Paul is assuring his living Thessalonian converts that the dead Thessalonian believers ("those who sleep in death," not "those who already have a resurrection body in heaven") will not be left out at the resurrection when Christ returns and raises the dead. Early Jews who believed in resurrection did not believe in a spiritual resurrection body assumed at death. To the contrary, as a text like Dan. 12:1–3 shows, they assumed that resurrection would happen when the dead are raised from the earth in a physical condition. And Paul follows that pattern clearly in 1 Cor. 15:20–23. He says that when Christ returns, the dead in Christ will be raised and receive the resurrection body like that of Christ, who was the firstfruits of the bodily resurrection—not before then. He does not say that those Christians who have already died, including some of the original eyewitnesses (cf. 1 Cor. 15:6), have already gotten resurrection bodies. Further, close attention to the grammar in 1 Cor. 15 is necessary. Paul is not contrasting a physical body with a spiritual body. He is talking about a body animated by life breath (*psychē*), like Adam was originally, and a body animated by the Holy Spirit. An adjective that ends in *-ikon* (*psychikon* in 15:44, 46) doesn't refer to the substance of which the body is made, but rather refers to the animating principle.[9] Likewise, *pneumatikon sōma* refers to a body animated by the Spirit, not a nonmaterial body (i.e., a spiritual body).

According to 2 Cor. 5:5, the Spirit is the **down payment** or guarantee that all this is true about the afterlife. At present we are at home in this body and away from the Lord, but there will be a time when we are away from this mortal frame and at home with the Lord. The presence of the Spirit here and now gives us confidence for the future about the things currently unseen. Frank Matera puts it this way: "Thus God prepared . . . believers for the general resurrection of the dead when he 'gave' them the gift of the Spirit that Paul describes as a 'pledge' [*arrhabōn*], the same concept he employed in 1:22."[10]

9. Contra Garland, *2 Corinthians*, 250–57, who is following Harris, *Second Epistle to the Corinthians*, 386–410.
10. Matera, *II Corinthians*, 123.

Everlasting Treasures in Clay Vessels

One of the enduring images that Paul draws on in this part of his discourse is that of clay jars being used to store something precious. In the Old Testament such vessels are the classic image of something that is fragile, easily broken, vulnerable, to be contrasted with something solid and lasting (see Job 4:19; Lam. 4:2, where in both cases the reference involves an analogy between such vessels and the human body). Amphorae were used to hold wine and oil, but also grains of various sorts. Sometimes, however, very precious things might be stored in jars, and even buried in the yard. Why? Because there were no banks as we know them in many places in the Roman Empire. Temples could be used for housing sacred or secular documents, jewels, precious stones, and more. But in Israel there was only one temple, in Jerusalem, and so people tended to store their precious items where they could readily have access to them as needed. The same was true of many of the more rural areas in the empire. Recall that many of the Qumran scrolls were stored in clay jars in caves above the Qumran site at the Dead Sea.

But here Paul is drawing an analogy between the human body with the light of God that dwells within the believer and a clay vessel with something precious in it. Paul stresses that our vessels are weak, vulnerable, fragile, but in one sense that is a good thing. If you've ever seen a first-century pottery lamp, you will know that the thinner the clay, the more light that gets out. For example, Paul believes that when people look at him (and ministers like him)—battered, in pain, with various scars—and yet see the light of God in his fragile and abused body, they will know that the power, the light, the glory come not from him but rather from God's light, God's Spirit, within him.

I once heard the story of the servant of a nineteenth-century prince and princess who lived in India near the Ganges River. Every morning the servant went down to the river with a yoke on his shoulder, carrying two clay vessels to the river to fill them up with water to be used in the palace for cleaning and other things. One morning, on the way to the river, the servant was astounded to overhear a conversation between the two clay vessels. One of them was bemoaning the fact that he had a crack that slowly leaked water, so that he never got back to the palace with a full load of water like the other vessel did. Hearing this, the servant interrupted the lamentation and said, "Have you not paid attention to the side of the path that you are on? On the way back from the river, the water you slowly lose has watered flowers that never would have grown or flourished without that leak or crack. There are no flowers on the other side of the path. So, not only do you provide some water for the palace, you provide flowers that I pick and give to the princess.

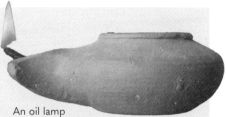

An oil lamp
J. Lekavicius / Shutterstock

Your flaws make you a more valuable vessel in the service of the prince and princess." This is precisely the way Paul views his own body. While outwardly he is wasting away and shows signs of abuse and weakness, inwardly he is being renewed day after day by the Spirit and the light of God's presence. We are meant to be visibly vulnerable people, such that when people look at us, they see the light of God in our all-too-mortal vessels.

This part of Paul's argument concludes with the reminder in 5:9–10 that we should always aim to behave in a way that pleases the Lord, because in the end we must all appear before the judgment seat of Christ to give an account of the deeds done in the body, and we will receive recompense for what we have done—either rewards for good behavior, or something not so good. See, for example, what Paul says in 1 Cor. 3:10–15 about ministers who escape as through fire if they have built their ministries on hay, stubble, and straw as opposed to gold, silver, and precious things. *Neither heaven nor salvation is a reward for good behavior, but there are rewards in heaven or at the judgment according to both Jesus and Paul.* The way Matera puts this is helpful: "Although what the justified have *done* will not justify them [since justification is by grace through faith], it will be the basis of the recompense they will receive."[11]

11. Matera, *II Corinthians*, 126.

The Opening Argument, Part Three

Paul the Ambassador

5:11So then, knowing the fear of the Lord, we persuade people, but to God we are made known, and, we hope, to your consciences as well. 12Not that we are commending ourselves to you again, but are giving you an opportunity for boasting about us, so that you may have [an answer] for those boasting about outward appearance and not in heart. 13For if we are out of our mind, it is for God; if we are in our right mind, it is for you, 14for the love of Christ constrains us, having reached this judgment—if one died for all, then all died, 15and he died for all, so that those who live should no longer live for themselves but for the one who died for them and was raised.

16From now on, then, we know no one according to the flesh. Even if we have known Christ according to the flesh, now we know him that way no longer. 17Therefore, if anyone is in Christ, a new creation. The old has passed away; behold, the new has come. 18But it is all from God, who has reconciled himself to us through Christ and has given us the ministry of reconciliation. 19That is, God was, in Christ, reconciling the world to himself, not reckoning their trespasses against them, and committing unto us the message of reconciliation. 20Therefore, on behalf of Christ we are ambassadors, since God is making his appeal through us. We plead on Christ's behalf, "Be reconciled to God." 21He

> made the one who did not know sin to be sin for us, so that in him we
> might become the righteousness of God. [6:1]Working together with him,
> we exhort you, "Don't receive the grace of God in vain." [2]For God says,
> "At an acceptable time I listened to you, and in the day of salvation I
> helped you." I tell you, now is the time of God's favor, now is the day of
> salvation.

At the beginning of this part of Paul's discourse he states plainly that he tries
to **persuade people** about the gospel. This admission is important because it
means that he does indeed use the art of persuasion, ancient rhetoric, but not
in the style or with the substance of Sophistic rhetoric, which is merely the art
of eloquence or the attempt to impress others for personal honor, gain, or fame.
Paul eschews all of that, and he trusts that the consciences of his audience know
that his real aims and purposes are good and godly.

When he talks about **commending** himself, he is not complimenting himself
or being self-congratulatory; rather, he means that he is offering his genuine
self as the servant of his audience once again, and he hopes that his audience
will be proud of what he does and has done for them. But also, he wants to give
his audience some reason, some ammunition, to fend off criticisms of him by
those who boast about **outward appearance** and put on a show rather than
speaking from the heart. He admits that this may appear to make him look
crazy to people inherently suspicious of orators of any kind, especially those who
aren't outwardly impressive. But the apostle adds that Christ's love compels or
constrains him to do what he does, even if it means that he looks ridiculous to
some.

The verb *synechō* is interesting (5:14). It occurs twelve times in the New
Testament (Matt. 4:24; Luke 4:38; 8:37, 45; 12:50; 19:43; 22:63; Acts 7:57; 18:5;
28:8; Phil. 1:23; and here at 2 Cor. 5:14). It can mean "hold together," or "press
hard," or "guard," or "constrain, control."[1] What Paul seems to mean is that "the
love of Christ, as expressed in the Gospel, has taken hold of Paul, puts limits
on his actions, and moves him in specific directions, constraining his course
of actions in the world, calling him to a self-sacrificial love patterned by Christ
himself. He has been boxed in and set on a particular course by the Gospel and
now lives only 'for him who died and was raised.'"[2]

1. Margaret Thrall suggests that "control" would be a more neutral translation because the
verb could be taken positively ("compel") or negatively ("constrain") (Thrall, *Second Epistle to the
Corinthians*, 1:408–9). The problem with a negative translation is that it's the love of Christ, or
possibly the love for Christ, that is causing things. If it is the former, then it is the example of the
self-sacrificial love of Christ consummated in his death that is motivating Paul.
2. Guthrie, *2 Corinthians*, 304.

Election and Salvation

Ancient cultures were basically little like modern ones in that although there were certainly individuals with their own personalities, the culture in itself was not given to modern ideas about individualism. Indeed, the dominant form of identity formation had to do with corporate identity, not individual personality. By this I mean that one's group identity was primary and one's individual identity was secondary. Perhaps you've noticed that people in the New Testament do not have, or do not mention, last names. "Christ" is not a last name, "Magdalene" is not a last name, and "Bar-Jonah" is a way of identifying Simon with a patronymic (i.e., in connection with his father), not as an individual. Again, group identity was primary, and this certainly affected the way Jewish people viewed the concept of election.

In the Old Testament there was an elect group—the Hebrews or the Israelites—and if you were part of that elect group, you got the benefits of it, but this is not the same as talking about being saved in a Christian sense as Paul does in 2 Cor. 5. In the New Testament Christ, rather than Israel, is the Elect One, which is made clear in Paul's letters by the phrase he constantly uses instead of the term "Christian": he says that believers are "in Christ." He is the Elect One, whom God chose before the foundation of the world to be the world's Savior, and if an individual is "in Christ," then they too are part of the elect group.

But even a moment's reflection will make clear that election is one thing and Christian salvation is another. Christ himself did not need to be saved. He is the one person for whom he didn't have to die! And yet he is the Elect One of God. In fact, election mostly has to do with God's historical purposes. For example, God chose the Persian king Cyrus to set the Israelites free from Babylonian bondage and exile. Cyrus is even said to be the one anointed for that task, the only named person in the Old Testament called *mashiah*, "messiah," God's "anointed one" (Isa. 45:1). This does not mean that Cyrus was a saved person. God, however, used him to accomplish divine ends and fulfill promises that God made to his people.

"Salvation" in the Old Testament does not have the full Christian sense that it obtains in Paul's letters and elsewhere in the New Testament. "Salvation" language in the Old Testament normally refers to being rescued from danger or from near-death experiences (see, e.g., Ps. 116, one verse of which Paul quotes in 2 Cor. 4:13), rescued from enemies, rescued from bondage and slavery, or even healed from disease. It doesn't refer to the gift of everlasting life in such cases, but rather has a more mundane meaning. Yes, sometimes it can refer to a spiritual sort of help or healing—for example, a restoration of an Israelite's relationship with God—but Christ is not mentioned, nor is everlasting life. It is clearly a this-worldly view of "salvation," and we see this in the Gospels as well. When a woman who has an issue of blood is healed, Jesus says to her, "Your faith has saved you" (Matt. 9:22), and clearly what he means is that her trust in Jesus has healed her body.[a]

Initial salvation, as Paul will say in various places, is by grace and through faith in Jesus, which establishes one in right relationship with God. Most Protestants tend to refer to this as justification by grace through faith. But that's not the end of the story, because there are three tenses to salvation: I *have been* saved (justification), I *am being* saved (sanctification, and working out corporately our salvation as God works in the midst of the community to will and to do [see Phil. 2]), and I *shall be* saved. Salvation is not complete until we are fully conformed to the image of Christ at the resurrection, when we receive a body immune to disease, decay, and death, like his. And importantly, all this happens because of Christ, and "in Christ," to create a permanent people of God.[b] We have already noticed that salvation is not by works, even by good works, but we have to answer for our behavior before the judgment seat of Christ (2 Cor. 5:10).

If, then, Christ died for all (and in place of all), why aren't all saved? It is not because God does not love the world, or does not want all to be saved; rather, it has to do with a human being freely responding to the gospel, becoming a new creature, dying to self, and following Christ, growing in grace, persevering to the end, and finally being conformed, even in the flesh, to the risen Christ. This outcome is not predetermined by God—Paul warns against apostasy—but there is the promise that nothing (other than ourselves), no third party, no circumstance, no malady or disease, no angel or devil can separate us from the love of God in Christ (Rom. 8:38–39).

Notice, finally, that the Holy Spirit is said to be the "down payment" (2 Cor. 5:5). The Spirit is the person who assures us and strengthens us to persevere, which we can do by God's grace and the Spirit's guidance and help. The Spirit is not the be-all and end-all of the Christian life, because we relate to the Father and the Son as well, and we come to the Father through Jesus the Son. The gifts and fruit of the Spirit are wonderful and much needed for the Christian life in this fallen world, but they are not the endgame; rather, they are the means by which we serve the Lord and his people and grow closer to God.

a. For a thorough discussion of the language of salvation in the Bible, including in Luke-Acts, see Witherington, *Acts of the Apostles*, appendix.
b. See the discussion in Witherington, *Biblical Theology*, 349–401.

In the midst of all this sort of ethical discussion, Paul adds that there is a person who **died for all** human beings, so that we might all **live** for him. Paul is, of course, referring to Christ, and notice that he does not affirm the notion of a limited atonement, with the Savior dying only for the elect. Here, in 5:15, **all** means *all*, just as the gospel calls everyone to die to self and live for Christ. But a bit more should be said about salvation and election at this point, which Paul will go on to stress involves a person leaving their old self behind and becoming a new creature or new creation, with the old self dead and gone.

Scholars have debated whether the phrase **known Christ according to the flesh** (5:16) refers to knowing the historical Jesus, and then they have asked: Did Saul of Tarsus in fact meet Jesus of Nazareth? Did he hear Jesus teach, perhaps in the temple in Jerusalem? Did he know about Jesus' trial and crucifixion? All of this is perhaps possible, since from Acts we learn that Paul grew up in Jerusalem and became a pupil of Gamaliel. But notice that he is still a young man when he observes the stoning of Stephen (Acts 7:58), the first Christian martyr. Whatever may have been the case in the past, Paul no longer evaluates Jesus in the same way he did in the past. He no longer evaluates Christ, or for that matter, anyone, from a merely worldly perspective, because the new creation has happened to Paul, and indeed to anyone who is **in Christ** or "in Christ Jesus"—the phrase that Paul uses, with slight variations, some seventy-six times in his letters to describe Christians. Indeed, he never uses the word *christianos* ("partisan of Christ" or "Christian"), instead preferring this pregnant phrase.

At a minimum, the phrase "in Christ Jesus" refers to those in relationship to Christ, but since Paul also talks about believers being part of the body of Christ, it seems likely that Paul sees the divine, omnipresent Christ as an incorporative personality. Believers are in him, but also Christ is in them (though "Christ in you, the hope of glory" is a phrase that occurs only once [Col. 1:27]). Paul much prefers the phrase about believers being incorporated into Christ.

It is interesting that both Jesus and Paul believed that people can change, something that was not a common belief in the ancient world. Most believed that each person is born with a certain personality and is stuck with it. It comes to light or develops over time, but it does not dramatically change at some point. The rhetorical question "Can a leopard change its spots?" was answered with an emphatic no. Yes, a person's nature and personality are *revealed* over time, but they don't change. Jesus and his followers were some of the first persons to really, fully believe that people could dramatically change for the better. Jesus talked about this in terms of being born again, or born from above (John 3:1–8).

Paul uses different language. He talks about new creation, or becoming a new creature with the old one having passed away. Notice the tense of that verb. Paul doesn't say that the old self "is gradually passing away"; he says **has passed**

away (5:17). What this amounts to is further explained in Rom. 8:1–2, where we learn not only that there is no condemnation for those "in Christ" but also that the Holy Spirit has set them free from the death grip that the ruling principle or law of sin and death had on their lives. If Christ has set you free from that by means of the Holy Spirit, you are free indeed.

It is precisely these kinds of beliefs about change, about salvation, about redemption, about reconciliation that fueled what amounted to the first intentionally evangelistic religion to change the world. The reasoning was clear: God desired all to be saved; Christ died and paid for the sins of the world; the world then could be saved from the bondage to sin; so everyone needed to hear and respond to this good news; and so suddenly, Paul and others were traversing the empire with this message, and it was producing remarkable results.

Rodney Stark estimates that in AD 90 there were at least 40,000 Christians in the Roman Empire, by AD 150 there were 218,000, and by AD 250 there were over a million.[3] Already at the beginning of the second century Pliny, writing from Bithynia to the emperor Trajan, is noting that there are a lot of them, and they will not be quiet.[4] This happened in part because of the strong commitment to evangelize one and all, but also because Christians married and had numerous children, and also redeemed slaves from bondage and adopted orphans, helped widows, fed the poor, and in short did whatever it took to lead people to Christ. It was definitely not all accomplished through preaching, though that was a very important part of it.

In the midst of all this, Paul brings up for the first time in 2 Corinthians the theme of **reconciliation**, which surprisingly is not a common theme in Paul's letters.[5] We should not think of this in terms of estranged marriage partners, as the term "reconciliation" is often used today. No, in antiquity the term usually was used in reference to being reconciled to people who were one's enemies or one's rivals (see, e.g., Rom. 5:10; Eph. 2:14–16; cf. 2 Macc. 1:5; 5:20; 7:33; 8:29), and in the main the language here is about being reconciled to God, not reconciliation between one or another group of human beings, although that is implied in Eph. 2:14–16 as well.

The point is that human beings, who have sinned and fallen short of God's glory, are alienated from God, and God through his ambassador or agent is the one initiating the attempted reconciliation by, in the first place, through the death of God's Son, paying the price for the sins that have separated people from

---

3. See Stark, *The Rise of Christianity*, chap. 1.

4. See the letter from Pliny to Trajan (and the reply) written in about AD 111 (Pliny, *Letters to Trajan* 10.96–97).

5. Despite Ralph Martin's best efforts to suggest that it is the heart of Pauline theology. See, e.g., Martin, *2 Corinthians*.

God. This notion that God takes the initiative to be reconciled to sinful human beings stands apart from the extrabiblical texts about reconciliation between humans, or human attempts to be reconciled to some deity. But notice that the phrase **Be reconciled to God** is an exhortation to those whom Paul has already addressed as believers. In short, they may have become estranged from God to some degree due to sin, or acceptance of false teaching, and God and Paul, as God's ambassador, want them back.

The term "ambassador" is appropriate, because in Paul's world **ambassadors** were the representatives of rulers tasked with negotiating peace treaties between warring factions or peoples. In part, Paul sees his own role as an apostle in this light. In fact, the Greek term *presbutēs* (cf. Eph. 6:20), when used in the Greek-speaking eastern end of the Mediterranean, referred specifically to the emperor's legate, sent to conclude peace treaties with conquered groups and reconcile them to their new social condition and situation.[6] The language of this passage clearly reflects the role of the ambassador in that context. What is likely implied by Paul's use of this language is that he sees himself as the ambassador of the real ruler of his world: not the emperor, but the Lord Jesus Christ.

Second Corinthians 5:21 is a theologically rich statement about Christ actually becoming the sin-bearer (cf. the Old Testament concept of the scapegoat in Lev. 16:10) so that we might **become the righteousness of God** in Christ. This is not likely about our being given right standing with God, or justification, in light of the verb used here. Like we have become new creatures, so too we have become the righteousness of God in Christ. Further, *this does not mean that Christ became our righteousness for us.*

No, when we are incorporated into the body of Christ, we have the sanctifying work of the Holy Spirit to conform our moral character to that of Christ, but this happens only "in Christ," which is to say in union with him and in the corporate body of Christ, the body of believers. The contrast in Rom. 5:19 is not about imputed righteousness as opposed to actual righteousness. The text itself in fact speaks of our being *made* righteous, just as human fallenness inherited as a result of Adam's sin made us actual sinners. So once more, the context in which we **become the righteousness of God** is by being in Christ, and through the internal working of the Spirit of God, whom Christ sent forth at Pentecost and who joined us to the body of Christ in the first place (see 1 Cor. 12:13).

Second Corinthians 6:1 is an important verse in this context because Paul has to urge his converts, **Don't receive the grace of God in vain**. Clearly, Paul thinks that some of the audience might do so, or may have already done so,

---

6. See Long, *II Corinthians*, 109, following A. Deissmann.

and that this is actually possible for persons who had initially been justified by grace through faith.

In 2 Cor. 6:2 we have a quotation from Isa. 49:8 (LXX). In context, the **acceptable time** is when God has acted for the rescue of his people, who are languishing in exile. That Paul says **now is the time of God's favor** ("now is the acceptable time" [NRSV]) refers to his belief that he lives in the eschatological time, when God's promises and prophecies are being fulfilled in Christ and in his followers and eschatological salvation is possible. So those who hear the gospel need to seize the moment and respond positively. If one reads Isa. 49:1–6, and indeed the whole of Isa. 49–53, it becomes clear that Paul sees not merely Christ but also himself in light of the discussion of the "servant" in those passages. Notice how in Isa. 49:1–6 the prophet presents his credentials like Paul does, but that same prophet was met with the kind of resistance that Paul has been experiencing as well, and he fears, "I have been laboring in vain" (49:4). However, God sees the prophet differently than the world does and honors and strengthens him (49:5–6). Paul is telling here very much the same tale about himself.[7]

---

7. See, rightly, Garland, *2 Corinthians*, 304–5.

The Opening Argument, Part Four

Paul's Trials and Tribulations

[6:3]In no way or respect giving anyone occasion for offense, so the ministry will not be blamed, [4]rather, in everything as God's ministers we commend ourselves, by great endurance in afflictions, in hardships, in difficulties, [5]in beatings, in imprisonments, in riots, in labors, in sleepless nights, in times of hunger, [6]by purity, by knowledge, by patience, by kindness, by the Holy Spirit, by sincere love, [7]by the word of truth, by the power of God, by the weapons of righteousness in the right hand and the left, [8]through glory and dishonor, through slander and good report, regarded as deceivers yet true, [9]as unknown yet recognized, as dying and yet behold we live, as being disciplined and yet not killed, [10]as grieving yet always rejoicing, as poor yet enriching many, as having nothing yet possessing everything. [11]Thus, we have spoken openly to you Corinthians; our hearts have been wide open. [12]We are not withholding our affection from you, but you are withholding yours from us. [13]As a fair exchange—I speak as to my children—open wide your hearts also.

There is an interesting back-and-forth between Paul feeling that he has to commend himself and his work for the Corinthians, yet at the same time trying not to pat himself on the back and appear to emulate the self-seeking and egocentric pseudo-apostles currently in Corinth. Notice that this theme of Paul and his coworkers commending themselves runs right through this discourse from beginning to end, starting with the first part of the first argument in 2 Cor. 3 (cf. 3:1; 4:2; 5:12; 7:11; 10:12, 18; 12:11). This is to be expected in a defense speech like this one, but some of this is deliberately ironic because Paul will be boasting about things that his opponents would never brag about: all sorts of hardships and sufferings—in short, what would normally be seen as signs of weakness, failure, lack of apostolic power or divine favor.[1]

One of the things one discovers, which is somewhat of a surprise, as we work through these multiple Pauline hardship catalogs in 2 Corinthians often stressing unfortunate incidents and even disasters, is that Paul had been beaten many more times than we might have deduced from the book of Acts, had been jailed early on more than the once mentioned in Acts (at Philippi), and seems to have had a contract put out on him with people pursuing him to get rid of him, both Jews and Gentiles, and he had taken many risks to cross rivers, climb mountains, and much more in order to share the gospel. Not many missionaries today can make *all* these sorts of claims, and Paul is only about halfway through his various missionary travels at most!

Here in 2 Corinthians we catch Paul in midstream of his ministry, so to speak, paddling hard to keep his converts on course, within the fold, discerning enough to reject false teaching and false teachers, and as true to the gospel as Paul himself has been. Paul was not prepared to abandon even a difficult group of converts and merely move on to a new audience, unlike some ministers then and now. In fact, if we look carefully, Paul was not a mere traveling evangelist. No traveling evangelist spends a year and a half in Corinth and then two and half years in Ephesus as Acts suggests. Paul wanted to make sure that a congregation was well established, not merely revived in a two-week evangelistic crusade. The apostle to the Gentiles was more like a church planter with perseverance than an evangelist or revival preacher in terms of how he preferred to operate.

This first catalog is something of a mixed bag, because it is not simply a tale of woe but also a tale of how Paul responded *positively* to his trials and tribulations. Notice that Paul is proactive, not reactive to what he has endured and prevailed over, not merely by his own strength of Christian character, his own patience, kindness, knowledge, but, as he says, by the help of the Holy Spirit. His message to all of us would be, "Don't leave home without being prepared to rely on the Holy Spirit." Second Corinthians 6:4–10 is a tour de force list of nine sufferings, eight virtues, then ten antitheses meant to show how that enduring

---

1. See Guthrie, *2 Corinthians*, 324–35.

and prevailing is obviously God working through Paul, because it happens even in and through Paul's various weaknesses. George Guthrie helpfully lines up the list into the manner of the ministry and the means, so "in purity" pairs with "in the Holy Spirit," "in knowledge" pairs with "in genuine love," "in patience" pairs with "in the word of truth," and "in kindness" pairs with "in the power of God."[2]

What this catalog of woes and responses shows is how skilled Paul is as a rhetorician, and it mirrors other similar lists by rhetoricians (cf. [Anaximenes of Lampsacus?], *Rhetoric to Alexander* 26.1435b.25–39; Cicero, *In Catilinam* 2.10.25; *Pro Scauro* 16.37; *Pro Caelio* 22.55).[3] In an honor-and-shame culture, one did not normally laud or list one's trials and tribulations, which normally were thought to bring shame on a person and show that person to be weak and contemptible in a culture that was highly competitive for honor and plaudits. But Paul's point is that the mentioning of such things demonstrates clearly that the all-surpassing power that has converted the Corinthians came *through* Paul but *from* God. This brings up an important point.

Unfortunately, I too often have heard ministers brag about how many people have been saved or come to Christ through this person or that person. But actually, if Paul himself can indicate that he converted no one but rather that God did it through Paul, then there is no excuse for ministers making this kind of boast today. This would be like a quill pen bragging that it had written twenty good plays by Shakespeare! God can write straight with a crooked stick. He can even speak truth through the mouth of Balaam's donkey. There is no room for hubris when one is a mere servant or slave or instrument in the hands of the Master.

The **weapons of righteousness**, as Paul calls them, are the Word and the Spirit. Notice that Paul is honest enough to say that in some of these trials he has been disciplined, put through the refiner's fire by God. Though God did not initiate the suffering and abuse, he could use it to discipline Paul and make him a better person, a better apostle, a more useful servant. While on the surface Paul might look like a bedraggled beggar and wanderer, in fact, however hungry or poor he might be at a given time, he counts himself as having all he needs. It will be useful to reflect for a bit on Paul's theology of "enough," which is the antithesis of the health-and-wealth gospel, the "God wants you to be materially rich" gospel. That would not be the view of the apostle who said, "The love of money is a root of all kinds of evil" (1 Tim. 6:10 NIV).

Sufferings, on the other hand, were a test of character, and on that score, Paul passed the test with flying colors. Instead of suffering making him bitter,

---

2. Guthrie, *2 Corinthians*, 329.
3. See the discussion in Keener, *1–2 Corinthians*, 188.

"I Can Endure All Things in Him"

In Phil. 4:11–13 we read the following: "I have learned to be content whatever the circumstances. I know what it is to be in need, and I know what it is to have plenty. I have learned the secret of being content in any and every situation, whether well fed or hungry, whether living in plenty or in want. For all things I have strength through him who empowers me." Too often, in our time especially, this last verse has been called the "superman verse," and mistranslated as "I can do all things through him who strengthens me." It has become the theme verse of some famous Christian professional athletes, such as Tim Tebow. But the context makes perfectly clear that this rendering is indeed a mistranslation.

Paul says that he has learned to be content whatever his circumstances, and we know perfectly well that some of those circumstances have been dire and involved lots of suffering. He has experienced the extremes of plenty and want and not let any of that change him or his course of ministry. The secret of being content regardless of one's circumstances is to rely on God, who strengthens the apostle and gets him through any and all circumstances whether good or evil, whether delightful or dire.

In short, this passage has *nothing* to do with a person being able to leap tall buildings in a single bound or accomplish all the desires of their self-centered heart. The so-called gospel that says "If you have enough faith and put God first, he will keep you well and make you rich" is emphatically repudiated by Paul's letters, especially 2 Corinthians and Philippians. In fact, amazingly, we will learn later in 2 Corinthians that God refused to remove the painful stake in Paul's flesh, some kind of physical problem causing pain, because God said to him, "My power is made perfect in your weakness; my grace is sufficient for you" (12:9). This is a message many Americans do not wish to hear or believe.

One more passage is worth mentioning briefly. When Jesus says, "Seek first the kingdom of God and his righteousness, and all these things will be added to you" (Matt. 6:33), he is not referring to whatever desires you may have in your heart. The context of this verse is the previous discussion about the necessities of life—food, shelter, clothing, length of life—and Jesus is saying that we need not worry about those necessities of life. If God cares for such needs even in the case of a sparrow, he also cares for such needs in human beings and will take care of us. This Paul came to believe with his whole heart, and so he preached the message that "godliness with contentment produces great gain" (1 Tim. 6:6).

N. T. Wright strikes exactly the right balance in his interpretation of this catalog passage:

> The extraordinary balance of the passage reveals the mark of genuine Christian authenticity. Christians sometimes talk as if life were simply a matter of glory, of celebration, of the Lord providing all our needs and everything going forward without a hitch. Nobody actually lives like that all the time . . . and the effort to go on believing in the face of the evidence can produce a double life, with all the dangers of hypocrisy and shallowness. Equally, some people—including some Christians—react so forcefully to a grinning, shallow, falsely cheerful spirituality that they make out that everything is gloomy and filled with trouble, a constant round of difficulty and frustration. Christian maturity gets the balance right. It isn't so much a matter of a bit of this and a bit of that; it's a lot of both and at the same time. And part of the task, not only of being a Christian, but leading a Christian community, is to be able to grieve and celebrate at the same time, to share the pain and joy of the world, and indeed the tears and the laughter of God.[a]

a. Wright, *Paul for Everyone: 2 Corinthians*, 69–70.

it made him better, as he relied more wholly on God in the person of the Holy Spirit to get him through it all.[4]

One of the main things one should definitely learn from this passage as a minister of any kind is that external perception is one thing, and the reality may be something quite different. Paul has been perceived by some as a deceiver, a huckster, as someone cleverly trying to pry money out of the Corinthians, as poor and needy, and even as dying. Yet the reality is that Paul does not have ulterior and personal motives when it comes to money; his trials and sufferings are not signs that God is against his ministry, but rather should be seen as testing or discipline. One wonders how often we have Paul's perspective on difficulties when things go wrong. Do we take it as a negative judgment on us personally or, rather, as something that doesn't come from God but that God can use for good in our life and ministry? Inquiring minds want to know. For sure, how we persevere through trials like Paul's says more about our Christian character than how we respond to successes does.

4. On suffering as a test of character, see Seneca, *Dialogues* 1.4.5. But unlike Seneca, Paul is no Stoic, merely enduring suffering and not allowing it to hinder him. On the contrary, he sees his suffering as filling up the sufferings of Christ and as bearing witness to his converts and having a positive effect on them. He has fully embraced the notion that a suffering Messiah who also rose from the dead is not only the Savior of the world, paradoxically enough, but also the paradigm for the follower of Christ. See Keener, *1–2 Corinthians*, 188–89.

The Price of Success

Money and resources have always been a flash point when it comes to a successful ministry. For this very reason, my fellow Charlottean Billy Graham kept his hands off the money made through his crusades, books, and so on. He was also instrumental in setting up an agency for evangelical churches that would help them to remain accountable in what they did with their resources. It is called the Evangelical Council for Financial Accountability, and if you are serving any kind of free church or independent church, you should look into this organization and sign up for its wise advice, counsel, and oversight. The temptation, especially in America, for ministers to give way to greed and self-aggrandizing practices is too great for them not to have a source of outside accountability, especially with so many TV preachers preaching the false health-and-wealth gospel ("God wants you to be never suffering and always rich"). Too many times, the downfall of perfectly good ministries and ministers has been caused by lack of accountability and lack of external counsel and monitoring. This is precisely why in 1–2 Corinthians Paul talks about (1) refusing patronage, (2) setting up representatives of his churches to handle the collection, and (3) demonstrating godliness with contentment whatever one's personal resources. Success in ministry from Paul's point of view has nothing to do with modern American visions of personal monetary success. Nothing at all. As the Bible reminds us, the heart turned in upon itself leads to selfish, self-centered behavior, which is morally wrong, spiritually dangerous, and deadly to a self-sacrificial ministry for the benefit of others.

2 CORINTHIANS 6:14–7:1

"But I Digress"

On Avoiding Entangling Alliances

> ^{6:14}Do not become partners with unbelievers, for what partnership is there between righteousness and lawlessness? Or what does light share in common with darkness? ¹⁵What agreement does Christ have with Belial? Or what part has a believer with an unbeliever? ¹⁶And what agreement does the temple of God have with idols? For we are the temple of the [only] living God. As God said, "I will dwell and walk among them, and I will be their God, and they will be my people." ¹⁷Therefore, "Come out from among them, and be separate from them," says the Lord. "Do not touch any unclean thing, and I will welcome you. ¹⁸And I will be a Father to you, and you will be sons and daughters to me," says the Lord Almighty. ^{7:1}So then, beloved, since we have these promises, let us cleanse ourselves from every impurity of the flesh and spirit, perfecting holiness out of reverence for God.

Unfortunately, this digression has a long history of misinterpretation. It has led whole groups of Protestants, such as the Amish, to withdraw from general society and live apart in their own little enclaves, with their own rules and community life, their own schools, a refusal to participate in voting or the military, and various other things. Some readers may remember the movie, starring Harrison Ford, *The Witness*, in which this very passage was quoted by a grandfather to ward off his grandson from touching an unclean thing, in this case Ford's gun, for the Amish are strict pacifists. But Paul is not talking about such things. As 1 Cor. 5:9–10 and other Pauline texts indicate, Paul expects his converts to live *in* the world without being *of* the world, or embracing its worldview. I like this translation of Rom. 12:2: "Don't let the world squeeze you into its mold" (J. B. Phillips).

Another one of the misreadings involves taking 2 Cor. 6:14 as if it were referring to believers marrying ("being unequally yoked" with) unbelievers. Here Paul is *not* talking about religiously mixed marriages; he's talking about avoiding idolatry and immorality. When Paul does talk about such a marriage in 1 Cor. 7:12–15, he does not advise the woman in question to separate from her pagan husband unless he wishes to depart, in which case she can let him go. Paul's basic view is not only that the holiness of the believer passes on to her child (the child is "holy" or "set apart"), but also that she might actually be a good influence on the husband and lead him to the Savior. So again, 2 Cor. 6:14–7:1 has nothing to do with religiously mixed marriages.

In fact, Paul is continuing a conversation he had with the Corinthians before, in 1 Cor. 8–10, about not dining in pagan temple dining rooms, where, Paul says, one encounters not just unbelievers but also a demon: the presence of a false and evil spiritual being masquerading as a god. The problem is severalfold.

It was not just a matter of having a meal with friends, and Paul had no problems with eating meat; however, doing so in the presence of an idol, in the presence of an evil being, a so-called god, was an act of false worship. So here Paul will remind his audience to stay away from pagan temple dinner feasts. That is the context in which the warning comes that **Christ** and **Belial** have nothing **in common**, and believers and unbelievers cannot share in common a meal in that sort of idolatrous setting. The issue is not *menu*, for Paul will also say in 1 Cor. 8–10 that believers can eat whatever they find in the meat market in Corinth, wherever it came from, unless of course one has a weak conscience and it violates one's conscience to do so.

Not menu but *venue* is the issue, which is also the case in the decree in Acts 15:22–29. There James, like Paul, does not want the new Gentile converts to scandalize Jews, who every Sabbath affirm their allegiance to the only living God and who abhor idolatry.[1] In short, this has nothing to do with withdrawing from secular society in general. Rather, it has to do with avoiding idolatry that is a bad witness to Jews and to Gentiles whom one wishes to embrace the gospel about Christ.

The key to rightly interpreting this digression is the question, **What agreement does the temple of God have with idols?** All the more so since Paul goes

---

1. See the detailed discussion of these passages in Witherington, *Conflict and Community*; also Witherington, *Acts of the Apostles*.

on to say that believers are **the temple of the [only] living God**. Imagine the temple of the Lord partnering with the temple of Asclepius or Apollo in Corinth! For Paul, this is unthinkable, hence his strong words here. In this matter of worship and spiritual fellowship, believers should not partner with unbelievers. This passage, then, is *not* a call to withdraw from the world. Rather, elsewhere Paul will encourage Christians to live in the world without being of the world. An evangelistic religion needs to know where to draw the line that believers shouldn't cross, and Paul draws it at the door of the pagan temple. The quoting of Isa. 52:11 in 2 Cor. 6:17 supports this interpretation, for that text tells Israel to come out from associations with unclean heathen and their unclean idols. They are to return from exile leaving behind the land and practices of idolatry.

But it is not just Isa. 52:11 that Paul resorts to in order to make clear that God dwells among his people and thus they are the temple of the living God. There is a catena of allusions and partial quotations, including Lev. 26:11–12 and Ezek. 37:27, about God dwelling in the midst of his people and being their God, and also Ezek. 20:41 and 2 Sam. 7:14, about God even being his people's spiritual father and their being his children. These latter texts reveal what God promises to do if his people separate themselves from idolatry and immorality.

The contrast between **righteousness** and **lawlessness** in 6:14 makes sense if we compare Rom. 6:19, where we have the same two words. The ongoing association with guilds that had their meals in pagan temples, in which the god was said to be present and was prayed to, is in Paul's view immorality, the opposite of righteousness, and at the same time is a rejection of God's fundamental law warning against idolatry.

In 2 Cor. 6:14 the word *koinōnia* is an important one, derived from the word *koinē*, which means "common" (as in Koine ["common"] Greek). But the term literally refers to a sharing of something in common with someone, not the result of that sharing, which could be called "fellowship." Paul is urging the audience not to share in common with their pagan friends or neighbors acts of pagan worship involving idolatry, and sometimes at such dinner parties in pagan temples sexually immoral acts were committed with some of the servants, as 1 Cor. 10:7 makes clear by its quotation of Exod. 32:6: "They sat down to eat and rose up to play."

The use of the term **Belial** to refer to Satan is rare in the New Testament; it is a Hebrew word that means "worthlessness" or "wickedness." David Garland suggests that it is used as a sort of name here, like the way the term "Christ" is used, to contrast two opposing personal beings.[2] This same term is used at Qumran for Satan (1QM [War Scroll] 13.11).

---

2. Garland, *2 Corinthians*, 335.

Further proof that the issue here is participation in idolatry with unbelievers is found in the citation at 6:16 from Lev. 26:12, Jer. 32:38, and Ezek. 37:27, and this is followed in 6:17 by a combination citation of Ezek. 20:34 and Isa. 52:11, which involves warning the people against idolatry and emphasizes the need to take the sacred vessels out of a pagan context. Again, pagan worship is the backdrop here. In 2 Cor. 6:18 we have another combination citation, involving Deut. 32:18–19 and 2 Sam. 7:14, which on first glance appears to be an odd combination. The former of these clearly refers to the abandoning of Yahweh for "strange gods." In its original context 2 Sam. 7:14 refers to Solomon and God's promise to David about establishing his throne. The original refers to his becoming God's son, and God his Father, but in Paul's paraphrase we hear about sons *and* daughters. But perhaps more likely Paul only has Deut. 32 in mind here, and not also 2 Sam. 7:14, for the latter text doesn't mention "sons" (plural) and daughters, but in the idolatry text in Deut. 32 we hear about sons and daughters who had rejected Yahweh for false gods. Overall, then, all these citations amount to a clear critique of the idolatry and immorality that were part of pagan worship, and which apparently some Corinthians still needed an exhortation about even though 1 Cor. 10 was rather clear on the matter.

Second Corinthians 7:1 makes clear that Paul takes these passages as promises that God intends to cleanse his people, but they too must cleanse their bodies and spirits from all such physical and spiritual defilement. This digression apparently was a necessary warning, because such behavior was still an ongoing problem at Corinth. There is no reason to see this passage as more than a digression. It has no epistolary features to suggest it is a separate letter, nor does it offer a subject alien to what Paul has said before in 1 Cor. 8–10. Rhetorical digressions were common in long speeches, especially if they addressed one of the ongoing and underlying problems that the audience needed to deal with. Such is clearly the case here.

Today as well, discerning ministers will not be oblivious to ongoing problems in their churches, which if not dealt with can fester and then blow up and become even bigger problems later. A good pastor and staff know how to diagnose the spiritual drift and temperature of their people, and what can be done in a careful, prayerful, and loving way to correct the problem. Sometimes this even requires tough love and discipline of some church member or members. Problems should not be ignored, and one must beware of passive-aggressive behavior by some church members who indirectly try to solve problems "without bothering the pastor." One must also beware of listening to one group in the church at odds with another group in the church. There will always be those who try to draw close to the pastor and give advice in order to promote their own agendas in the church. All such communications must be evaluated carefully and critically, listening to a variety of voices, not just a few. But unfortunately, sometimes a new pastor doesn't have time to do all this, as he or she has not yet had time to get to know the people well. This becomes a major problem especially in a large church, where it is simply impossible for the ministers to know all the members well, however much they may try to do so.

I was pastoring four country churches at once in the early 1980s at the beginning of my pastoral work after my doctoral work abroad, and I went to my very first church board meeting at one of these churches not knowing that a crisis had been brewing for some time. Two families were at odds with each other as to who should run the church music program and be the Sunday school superintendent. All of a sudden, this situation blew up at my first board meeting across the long table where we were all sitting. Both sides expected me to side with them on the matter, but I didn't know either family very well yet, so after the blowup at the meeting, I started asking other members of the church what was going on and how long this had been festering.

Then I went to both the feuding families and talked with them, and urged them to stay and work things out, since this tiny church could hardly afford to lose members. The root of the matter was jealousy. One set of parents wanted their daughter to do the music ministry, and the other set of parents had their children already doing it and, frankly, doing it well. The end result was that the jealous parents left the church, and I could not persuade their children (husband and wife) to stay, as it would create too much drama with their parents. The parents left because I did not reject what the congregational majority said about the matter. Sometimes, crises do not involve reconciliation and healing between those at odds with one another in the church. Sometimes, one has to lose some members in order to carry on doing positive ministry, especially if one is too new in the situation to know the persons well enough to make a judgment.

"As I Was Saying"

Joy and Sorrow from Titus's Report

^{7:2}Make room for us in your hearts. We've wronged no one, corrupted no one, defrauded no one. ³I don't say this to condemn you, since I have already said beforehand that you are in our hearts to die together and live together. ⁴I use free speech with you; I have great pride in you. I'm filled with encouragement, overflowing with joy in all our afflictions. ⁵For in fact when we came into Macedonia, our flesh had no rest. Instead, we were troubled in everything, conflicts without, fears within. ⁶But God, who comforts the downcast/humble, comforted us by the arrival of Titus, ⁷and not only by his arrival but also by the comfort he received from you. He told us about your yearning, your sorrow, your zeal for me, with the result that I rejoiced even more. ⁸For even if I grieved you with my [severe/sorrowful] letter, I don't regret it, and even if I regretted it since I saw that the letter grieved you, yet only for a while. ⁹I now rejoice, not because you were grieved, but because your grief led unto repentance. For you were grieved according to God, in order that you not experience any loss from us. ¹⁰For grief according to God produces a repentance that leads to salvation without regret, but grief of this world produces death. ¹¹For behold how this grief according to God produced such earnestness in you—what a defense, what indignation, what fear, what deep longing, what zeal, what justice! In everything you showed yourself to be pure in this matter. ¹²So even though I wrote to you, not because of the one who did wrong or the one

who was wronged, it was so that your devotion to us might be made plain to you before the sight of God. [13]By all this we are encouraged.

In addition to our own encouragement, we were especially delighted to see how happy Titus was, because his spirit has been refreshed by all of you. [14]I had boasted to him about you, and you have not embarrassed me. But just as everything we said to you was true, so our boasting about you to Titus has proved to be true as well. [15]And his affection for you is all the greater when he remembers that you were all obedient, receiving him with fear and trembling. [16]I am glad I can have complete confidence in you.

There are two ways one can view this passage, either as a continuation of the "narration" before the argumentation began in 2 Cor. 3[1] or as the conclusion of the first major argument. But the backstory, in this case the one verse that tells of Titus coming and reporting, is brief, and the vast majority of this paragraph wraps up the discussion of, on the one hand, affliction, grief, worry and, on the other hand, relief and comfort from the earlier argument, so it is better to see this as the conclusion of the first major argument before Paul moves on to a new subject, the collection for the Jerusalem church in 2 Cor. 8–9.

So, this paragraph is in fact the conclusion of the various parts of the first argument and comes only after the brief digression reaffirming the previous teaching about idolatry, particularly in 1 Cor. 10. The digression was necessary because evidently Titus reported that there were still problems with some Corinthians going to pagan temples. It would be difficult, especially for the more socially elite Corinthian Christians, like Erastus the city treasurer (see Rom. 16:23), to simply stop going to pagan temple dinner parties, since that was where one made friends, gained votes, made business deals, set up family alliances, and more. Religion and politics were always intertwined in the Greco-Roman world, but Paul (in enforcing James's decree in Acts 15:22–29 so that Jewish followers of Christ would not be harmed and the witness to Jews would not be scandalized and stifled) had to take a strong stand and draw a firm line on attending such feasts.[2]

We are not sure what Paul is talking about when he refers to **the one who did wrong** and **the one who was wronged** (7:12), but the immediate context may favor the view that Paul is the wronged person, as the whole first part of 2 Corinthians might suggest. One might wonder as well if **the one who did wrong** refers to the individual who repented and should now be forgiven and

1. See Keener, *1–2 Corinthians*, 198–99.
2. See Witherington, *Conflict and Community*, 186–230.

shown mercy. This also would make sense in light of what has come before in this discourse. On the other hand, the very end of this paragraph suggests that one Corinthian did something wrong to another convert in Corinth and then was corrected by various of the leaders there, and Paul is encouraging forgiveness and mercy now that genuine repentance has happened.

In an important article John Barclay provides an insightful contrast between the Corinthian congregations and those in Thessalonica.[3] Barclay notices that there is quite a contrast between how the Thessalonians have interacted with and related to non-Christians in town and how the Corinthians have done so. The Thessalonians have endured persecution and even lost some members because of it and seem to have withdrawn into a sort of holy huddle for self-protection, whereas the Corinthians, at least the Gentiles among them, seem still fully integrated into Corinthian life, including attending pagan dinner parties not only in homes but also in pagan temples.

Barclay concludes that the Corinthian church "is not a cohesive community but a club, whose meetings provide important moments of spiritual insights and exaltation, but do not have global implications of moral and social change. The Corinthians could gladly participate in this church as one segment of their lives. But the segment, however important, is not the whole and the center. Their perception of their church and of the significance of their faith could correlate well with a life-style that remained fully integrated in Corinthian society."[4] While this may be too negative an assessment in regard to some of the converts in Corinth, particularly the Jewish ones who did not go to pagan temples even before they embraced Christ, on the whole this seems on target. They have not been doing a good job of distinguishing between being "in the world" and being "of the world," remaining in the embrace of a pagan worldview.

So Paul is relieved that some of them at least have repented of their harsh evaluation of him and want to have a positive relationship with their apostle, but they are also anxious that he will come and condemn them for their sins and mistakes. And Paul wants to assure them that they are on the right track now, since he believes that Titus's report is true, and that report causes Paul to rejoice. John Chrysostom says of this passage where Paul has wounded his spiritual offspring but it led to repentance, "Like a father who watches his son being operated on, Paul rejoices not for the pain being inflicted but for the cure which is the ultimate result. He had no desire to cause harm for its own sake" (*Homilies on Second Corinthians* 15.1). But something more needs to be said about repentance.

---

3. See Barclay, "Thessalonica and Corinth," 50–71.
4. Barclay, "Thessalonica and Corinth," 71.

"Repentance," in Greek *metanoia*, and its cognates involve more than just feeling guilty or sorry about something that one has said or done. Repentance involves not merely a recognition that someone has done something wrong but also a rejecting of those past words or actions and a resolve to go in a different direction in the future. It involves not merely a change of mind or feelings; it involves a change in subsequent behavior. This is precisely why Paul is able to talk about the audience's justice in rebuking the person who had hurt Paul. This is also why as time went on the call for repentance was coupled with the call for confession, because public confession, not just to God but to other believers (see James 5:16), makes you accountable to never go there again, never say or do that again, because other believers will hold you responsible for your actions. This is precisely why John Wesley set up weekly, gender-specific band meetings where the question was asked, "What sins have you committed this week that you know of?" Confession was expected to go on, each week, to "keep short accounts with God and each other." Wesley did not think that confessing to a priest or a minister was sufficient or necessary, since James 5:16 suggests otherwise.

If Paul sounds to you a bit like a worried, and even nagging, parent in this passage, you are right. Paul's converts are indeed his surrogate children, and sometimes he addresses them that way as well, partly because of his deep love for them, but partly also because, as he implies in Gal. 4:19, he is their spiritual mother who gave birth to them by means of the Word and the Spirit. This passage mentions grief and relief a good deal, with the relief coming only after Titus gets back to Macedonia and gives Paul his report. The other side of this coin that reads "distress, worry, grief" is comfort, the kind only God can give. Paul speaks about worldly grief as opposed to godly grief, and surely the latter is what Paul is referring to here, as it has to do with being deeply concerned for the spiritual well-being of his converts. Worldly grief, says Paul, leads to death. I suspect that he is talking about the kind of soul-destroying grief where someone says, "I am worried to death about you." This is not a good kind of grief, for it only does harm to the one feeling it, and it does not really help the person they are worried about. Most ministers, then and now, would advise that instead of just worrying, one should just pray. That at least is a soul-affirming activity. But what does godly grief look like? First Thessalonians 4:8–13 deals with this contrast, and Paul reminds his converts that they are not to grieve like those who have no hope, not least because they have been given the gift of everlasting life, and they have a future that involves resurrection. But an illustration of what godly grief looks like may be helpful at this juncture (see the sidebar "Good Grief").

Paul has talked about reconciliation being an important part of salvation, and in this case the apostle no doubt felt it crucial that he be truly reconciled with his converts before he broached the subject of the collection. You really can't

Good Grief

My wife and I have known grief. Twelve years ago, we suddenly lost our thirty-two-year-old daughter, Christy, to a pulmonary embolism. One day she was alive and with us celebrating my sixtieth birthday, and shortly thereafter she was found dead on the floor of her house, with her two dogs lying beside her. Honestly, there are few more difficult things to cope with in life than the sudden loss of a child, and I wrote a brief book for *Christianity Today* about dealing with this, called *When a Daughter Dies*. It is a hopeless feeling to not be there for your child when they are struggling or not well, and as I read Paul's conclusion in 2 Cor. 7:2–16, I think that he could identify with this feeling of concern and even dread. But there is a difference between dreading the worst and then being reassured and, by contrast, getting the phone call that says your daughter is gone—unexpectedly, suddenly, shockingly. I got that phone call, and then I had to tell my wife what had happened. In fact, Christy had been dead for over a day before she was found by a friend in Durham, North Carolina. Godly grief in our case meant thanking God for the life of our firstborn child and remembering all the good times. We realized that life is a gift, the life of a child is a gift, and we were not *owed* more years with her. So, we celebrated the thirty-two years we had with Christy. We had the joyful "Widor Toccata" played at her funeral, and we sang "Joyful, Joyful, We Adore Thee." We did not grieve like those who have no hope of a positive afterlife for Christy and for ourselves.

But I have had to minister to people when I was a pastor who had worldly grief, and it quite literally killed them, so Paul's saying about worldly grief being associated with death is absolutely true. There was a seventeen-year-old boy whose family attended my church and the country Baptist church down the road. One evening he was stopped by the police, and he had some marijuana on him, and suddenly he pulled out a gun and shot himself in the head. This tore up the family, especially the father, who took to heavy drinking, and his worldly grief got so heavy, that exactly one year to the day after his son took his own life, the father did the same. In that situation, all I knew to do was to love the remaining family members, put my arms around them, and say positive things about what the afterlife brings to those who are in Christ, without preaching that individual into heaven, or somewhere else. Funerals are for the living, not really for the dead, and comfort is what must be offered in some form, without pretending to be the final judge of someone else's life, especially someone you knew only slightly.

To be honest, I was worried about what the fundamentalist Baptist preacher in their home church was going to say at that second funeral. He got up and read from the end of the book of Acts about Paul's shipwreck on Malta, and I wondered where in the world this message was going. He then commenced to talk about the storms of life, and how it could end tragically, and after a while he said, "Unless you too have gone on the spiritual journey with the man in the casket, and experienced his life and the depths of his grief, you are in no position to judge his character or to say where he is now in the afterlife. You should mourn with those who mourn, and remember the words of Jesus: 'Blessed are those who mourn, for they shall be comforted.'" I was so relieved after this message was given, and we all did our best to comfort the family.

We can conclude this section with another quote from my favorite early interpreter of Paul's letters, John Chrysostom: "Worldly sorrow [involves] regret for the loss of money, reputation, and friends. That kind of sorrow merely leads to greater harm, because the regret is often a prelude to a thirst for revenge. Only sorrow for sin is really profitable" (*Homilies on Second Corinthians* 15.2). Just so, and this was all the more the case in a culture that believed in reciprocity, payback both positive and negative. It was a culture in which repentance, forgiveness, and grace were alien concepts by and large.

ask people for money if they are estranged from you, angry with you, think that you have bad and selfish motives. So, reconciliation was an important first step before Paul could address the collection in his second argument in 2 Cor. 8–9. Near the very end of Paul's earlier major letter, at 1 Cor. 16:1–4, he said this: "Now about the collection for the Lord's people: Do what I told the Galatian churches to do. On the first day of every week, each one of you should set aside a sum of money in keeping with your income, saving it up, so that when I come no collections will have to be made. Then, when I arrive, I will give letters of introduction to the men you approve and send them with your gift to Jerusalem. If it seems advisable for me to go also, they will accompany me" (NIV). Second Corinthians 8–9 is a continuation of that exhortation.

Argument Two

"Now, about That Money for the Jerusalem Church"

^{8:1}We want you to know, brothers and sisters, the grace of God that was given to the assemblies of Macedonia. ²During a great trial of affliction their abundant joy and their extreme poverty overflowed in a wealth of generosity on their part. ³I bear witness that according to their power, and even beyond their power of their own accord, ⁴they begged us earnestly for the privilege of sharing in the ministry to the saints, ⁵and not just as we had hoped. Instead, they gave themselves first to the Lord, and then through God's will also to us. ⁶So, we urged Titus that just as he had begun, so he should complete among you also this gift.

⁷Now since you excel in everything—in faith and speech and knowledge and all diligence and in your love for us—excel also in this gift. ⁸I am not saying this as a command; rather, through the diligence of others I am testing the genuineness of your love. ⁹For you know the grace of our Lord Jesus Christ, though he was rich, for your sake he became poor, so that by his poverty you might become rich. ¹⁰And in this I give advice, for it is profitable for you, who began last year not only to do something but also to want to do it.

¹¹Now also, finish the task, so that just as there was [then] an eager desire, thus also [now] there may be a completion according to what you have. ¹²For if the eagerness is there, the gift is acceptable according to what a person has, not according to what he does not have. ¹³Not that there should be relief for others and affliction for you, but it is a

question of equality. [14]At the present time your surplus is available for their need, so that their abundance may in turn meet your need, in order that there may be equality. [15]As it is written, "The person who had much did not have too much, and the person who had little did not have too little."

[16]Thanks be to God, who put the same concern for you into the heart of Titus, [17]for he welcomed our exhortation, and being very diligent went out to you by his own choice. [18]We have sent him with the brother who is praised among all the assemblies for his gospel ministry; [19]and not only that, he was also appointed by the assemblies to accompany us with this gracious gift we are transmitting for the glory of the Lord himself and to show our eagerness to help. [20]We are taking this precaution so that no one will criticize us about this large sum we are transmitting. [21]Indeed, we are giving careful thought to do what is right before the Lord but also before human beings. [22]We have also sent with them our brother. We have often tested him in many circumstances and found him to be diligent and now even more diligent because of his great confidence in you. [23]As for Titus, he is my partner and coworker for you. As for our brothers, they are the apostles of the assemblies, the glory of Christ. [24]Therefore, show them the public proof, before the assemblies, of your love and our boasting about you.

[9:1]Now concerning the ministry to the saints, it is unnecessary for me to write to you, [2]for I know your eagerness, and I boast about you to the Macedonians. Achaia has been ready since last year, and your zeal has stirred up most of them. [3]But I am sending the brothers so that our boasting about you would not prove to be empty words, and so that you would be ready just as I said. [4]Otherwise, if any Macedonians would come with me and find you unprepared, we, not to mention you, would be put to shame in that situation. [5]Therefore, I considered it necessary to urge the brothers to go on ahead to you and arrange in advance the generous benefit you promised, so that it indeed will be ready as a benefit, and not as an extortion.

[6]The point is this: the one who sows sparingly will also reap sparingly, and the person who sows generously will also reap generously. [7]Each person should do as he has decided in his heart, not reluctantly or out of compulsion, since God loves a cheerful giver. [8]And God is able to make every gift overflow to you, so that in every way, always having all you need, you may excel in every good work. [9]As it is written, "He distributed freely; he gave to the poor; his righteousness endures forever."

> [10]Now the one who provides seed for the sower and bread for food will also provide and multiply your seed and increase the harvest of your righteousness. [11]You will be enriched in every way for all your generosity, which through us produces thanksgiving to God. [12]For the ministry of this liturgy / religious service is not only supplying the needs of the saints but also overflowing through many thanks to God; [13]because of the proof provided by this ministry, they will glorify God for the obedience of your confession of the gospel of Christ, and for your generosity in sharing with them and with everyone. [14]And as they pray on your behalf, they will have deep affection for you, because of the surpassing grace of God in you. [15]Thanks be to God for his indescribable gift!

It may come as something of a surprise to you, but the one topic that comes up most regularly in the capital Pauline letters is the collection for the Jerusalem church. It is mentioned briefly in Galatians as a request from the pillar apostles, or Jerusalem leaders, to remember the poor as Paul evangelizes the Gentiles. It comes up again at the end of 1 Corinthians, and then here in the middle of 2 Corinthians at considerable length, and then yet again in Rom. 15. Paul seems to see getting money together from his largely Gentile converts to give to the Jewish Christ-followers in Jerusalem and Judea as a top priority. Why?

We know that grain shortages happened in the eastern Mediterranean from time to time, in part because conditions in Egypt, the real breadbasket in the region, could lead to periodic famine. We also know that Rome itself focused on and took the lion's share of the harvest in Egypt for the dole in the capital. The province of Judea had to fend for itself in such times. We also learn from Acts 6:1–7 that while the number of converts to Christ was growing in Jerusalem, at the same time their most vulnerable members, widows, apparently were not being taken care of by the Jewish community in general, perhaps being cut off from the dole in Jerusalem and from the care that the larger community normally undertook for widows and orphans based on the Old Testament mandates (cf. Exod. 22:22–25). Notice that this very matter is on James's mind in James 1:27. So, there is this practical need that Paul has been asked to help with and is determined to do something about. But is that all there is to it?

The Letter to the Romans suggests that the answer is no. Near the end of that letter Paul says this:

> Now, however, I am on my way to Jerusalem in the service of the Lord's people there. For Macedonia and Achaia were pleased to make a contribution for the poor among the Lord's people in Jerusalem. They were pleased to do it, and

indeed they owe it to them. For if the Gentiles have shared in the Jews' spiritual blessings, they owe it to the Jews to share with them their material blessings. So after I have completed this task and have made sure that they have received this contribution, I will go to Spain and visit you on the way. (Rom. 15:25–28 NIV)

Paul seems to see the collection as a form of payback or reciprocity, since the gospel has come to the Gentiles from Jewish Christians like Paul and Peter, whose base is, of course, Jerusalem. Furthermore, Paul seems to have a concern that unity in Christ between Jews and Gentiles is not happening like it should, with the largely Gentile house churches taking on a life of their own, with Jewish Christians being a minority in them. Notice how Paul has to exhort the Gentiles not just in Rom. 14, but also earlier in 1 Cor. 8–10, not to disparage Jewish Christians who refuse to eat idol meat, or go to dinner parties in pagan temples, or for that matter participate in the regular religious festivals during the year in cities like Corinth, Ephesus, Thessalonica, and Philippi.

And at the beginning of the whole process, in Gal. 2, Paul expresses a deep concern that he might have been running in vain, doing mission work to no good end if the Jerusalem church didn't in fact give him the right hand of fellowship and the endorsement to go ahead and do this mission, a mission originally commissioned only by the Antioch church. Paul was not interested in starting a new religion for Gentiles only. And there were conservative Pharisaic Jewish Christians who had come to Antioch, and then to Galatia, and wanted to make sure that Paul's Gentile converts became full-fledged Jews, getting circumcised and keeping the Mosaic covenant. The compromise in Acts 15, endorsed by James, apparently put a stop to that effort, but that then raised this question: What *is* the relationship between the largely Jewish community of followers of Jesus in Israel, particularly Judea, and the largely Gentile communities of Christ-followers elsewhere? How could this growing religious movement be bound together as one entity? Paul not only saw the collection as a way to show the legitimacy of his Gentile mission to the skeptical in Jerusalem and elsewhere, but also saw it in an eschatological light, which is what Rom. 15 definitely suggests. Consider this passage:

Accept one another, then, just as Christ accepted you, in order to bring praise to God. For I tell you that Christ has become a servant of the Jews on behalf of God's truth, so that the promises made to the patriarchs might be confirmed and, moreover, that the Gentiles might glorify God for his mercy. As it is written:

"Therefore, I will praise you among the Gentiles;
    I will sing the praises of your name."

Again, it says,

> "Rejoice, you Gentiles, with his people."

And again,

> "Praise the Lord, all you Gentiles;
> let all the peoples extol him."

And again, Isaiah says,

> "The Root of Jesse will spring up,
> one who will arise to rule over the nations;
> in him the Gentiles will hope." (Rom. 15:7–12 NIV)

This catena of quotations comes from 2 Sam. 22:50, Ps. 18:49, Deut. 32:43, Ps. 117:1, and Isa. 11:10. Paul sees the Gentile mission as the fulfillment of the promise that God made to Abraham that he would be a light to the nations and the sign that finally in the eschatological age the Gentiles would come streaming to Zion (see Zech. 8:20–23) bearing gifts of gratitude for their inclusion in the people of God, something that Jesus himself seems to have predicted (Matt. 8:10–11). In short, the collection is seen as a vehicle to show that the Gentile mission without imposing the Mosaic covenant on Gentiles is the right move, and that the prophecies are coming true, and that the Jewish and Gentile parts of the Christ movement need to stand together when they face challenges of all sorts, including food challenges. But did this collection accomplish all that Paul had hoped?

Acts 20:4, which lists a considerable number of Paul's converts accompanying Paul with this large gift, and Acts 21 do not suggest that things turned out well in Jerusalem, though initially Paul and those carrying the collection from various places were well received, and James suggested that some of the money be used to support Nazarite vows in the temple. Did some of the conservative and more skeptical Jewish Christians see the money as a polite bribe for them not to impose the Mosaic covenant on Gentiles and simply accept Paul's view of that mission? We cannot be sure.

But what we do know from the rest of Acts is that when Paul was taken prisoner and was in Caesarea Maritima under house arrest, apparently no one from Jerusalem came to Paul's defense, and eventually Paul had to appeal to the emperor to get out of that situation. Apparently, the apprehension that Paul felt when he wrote in Rom. 15:31 that the collection might not be accepted in

Jerusalem and that the unbelievers there might be angry and after him was not a mere apprehension; it was a preview or foreshadowing of what was to come.

But here, in 2 Cor. 8–9, Paul is full of hope that the collection will be a clear sign of the genuine nature of his Gentile mission and the desire of the Gentiles to be one in Christ with Jewish followers of Jesus (see Gal. 3:28). He says that he doesn't want to order the Corinthians to comply, but instead he is testing the genuineness or authenticity of their love, presumably for the Lord and the gospel, not for Paul in particular, but that could be implied as well. In any case, since Paul did not organize collections for other congregations suffering from famine or persecution, it seems clear that he saw special spiritual significance in the uniting of his churches with the mother church in Jerusalem, a concrete example and symbol of Jew and Gentile united in Christ.[1] With this in mind, we can look at the details of these chapters.

The Greek word *charis*, which we regularly translate as "grace," in fact has as its most basic meaning "gift."[2] Of the 156 occurrences of this word in the New Testament, a full 100 of them are in Paul's letters. He is the preeminent theologian of grace in the New Testament.[3] And as N. T. Wright points out, in the whole of 2 Cor. 8–9 Paul never once uses any of the Greek words for "money." He talks instead indirectly about the *charis*, the **gift** (8:1, 4, 6–7, 19; 9:14).[4] In fact, Paul engages in a bit of wordplay, as in a couple of places the term seems to have the more theological meaning "grace." This delicate approach may be because money was not merely a delicate subject; it was a sore subject with the Corinthians ever since Paul refused payment for his oratory and help (see 1 Cor. 9). And now, is he asking the Corinthians for money for a group of people in a foreign country whom they have never met?

And there may even be a further problem: Roman Gentiles with anti-Semitic ideas. Such ideas, sadly, were rife among Romans, and we must remember that Corinth had been made a Roman colony, ruled by Romans like Gallio the proconsul. Paul had much to overcome to achieve his goal of all his Gentile churches contributing freely to the collection. If we ask the question of why exactly these chapters are here, and why Paul leaves his arguments about the "super-apostles" until 2 Cor. 10–13, there are at least two plausible answers. First, this letter may have been composed in stages, with a report coming to him later about the pernicious influence of these rival false teachers. Second, more probably, Paul is following the usual rhetorical protocol of leaving the

---

1. See Garland, *2 Corinthians*, 388–89.
2. See the wonderful detailed study of this word by Barclay, *Paul and the Gift*.
3. Contrast this with the fact that *charis* occurs in the first chapter of the Gospel of John and never again in that Gospel.
4. Wright, *Paul for Everyone: 2 Corinthians*, 84–85.

bone of contention, the biggest problem, until well after he has established or, in this case, reestablished rapport with his audience and feels that he is on firm enough footing to attack the problem head-on. Rhetorically speaking, this approach can be called *insinuatio*, whereby one hints at the big problem early in the discourse (see the thesis statement in 2:17 and elsewhere) and then attacks it head-on at the end of the discourse, very much as Paul does in 1 Cor. 15.[5]

You might also have thought that Paul had a lot of guts to be asking for money after all of the trauma that this very letter reflects in his rocky relationship with the Corinthians. And yet Paul presses on, so important is the collection to his overall ministry. Paul's first masterstroke is to tell the Corinthians about the generosity that the Macedonian churches showed at the very time they were experiencing poverty. This is a shaming technique that could be very effective in a culture where obtaining honor and avoiding shame was a major preoccupation.

Unlike the Macedonians, the Corinthians don't seem to have lacked for resources, and so Paul is also invoking the ancient love for rivalry competitions. We must remember that at Isthmia, the Corinthians had biannual Olympics-style games in which people's fervor for competition was brought to fever pitch, and Paul seems surely to have been there during at least one cycle of those games, making tents for the visitors coming to stay for a while and watch the competitions.

The Macedonians gave not only according to their means but beyond their means, even begging to be allowed to contribute to the ministry to the saints. Here, and in some other places as well, Paul uses the term "holy ones" or "saints" to refer to the Jewish Christians in Jerusalem who need help. This may be because the term "Jew" had a negative valence with many Gentiles, and in an appeal for money, you don't stir up people's prejudices. Rather, you appeal to the better angels of their nature, in this case using the other term that keeps coming up in this discussion: "generosity." Paul even implies that the Macedonians did what they did as a stimulus for others, in this case Corinthians who had already begun to collect funds, to be likewise prompted to give generously and finish their collecting.

Second Corinthians 8:7–8 shows that Paul is a master at rhetoric. He flatters the audience that they are good at faith, at oral discourse, at knowledge, and at eagerness for various things, and then he says, **Not that I am commanding you to finish the collection, but simply testing your genuineness**. This is what we call making them an offer that they dare not refuse, unless they want to lose face, lose honor in the sight of their fellow believers both in Corinth and elsewhere.

5. On which, see my former doctoral student Timothy Christian's excellent thesis now published as *Paul and the Rhetoric of Resurrection*.

The eyes of the larger body of Christ are watching! It is worth noting that the economy in Corinth was doing very well in the middle of the first century, with lots of trade and business coming its way from its two seaports. Corinth was the stopping place for all sorts of merchants going east and west. So, it is likely that various Corinthians could well afford to give generously to the collection.

Were this not enough, Paul plays his christological trump card at 8:9. Christ, who had all the riches of heaven (see Phil. 2:5–11), did not take advantage of them but instead self-sacrificially committed himself to being a poor human being, out of love for lost humankind, so that they might be saved, be enriched by the gospel of redemption and reconciliation.

Again, at verses 10–11, Paul says that he is just giving his advice: "Finish what you started." But notice that he also tells them to give according to their means. If you are earnest in giving, it's not the amount of the gift that primarily matters, so one should give according to what one has, not according to what one doesn't have.

Verses 13–14 bring us to this crucial word *isotēs*, which does indeed mean **equality**. Paul boldly uses this term elsewhere, in Col. 4:1, to talk about masters and slaves being equals in the body of Christ![6] Abundance in one part of the assembly of God should supply a lack in another part, so there is a fair balance; and if the reverse were to happen, the Jerusalem church should supply the lack in Corinth. This seems to be a kind of sharing that already existed within the church in Jerusalem according to Acts 2:44–45 ("They shared all things in common") and 4:32 ("No one claimed exclusive right to what they had, but shared everything they had").

This chapter of 2 Corinthians has, at verse 15, a reminder from Exod. 16:18, from the story about manna from heaven in which each person had enough but not too much. Paul is suggesting that God's plan and desire are for equality, not wealth over here and poverty over there among his people. While the arm-twisting in this rhetorical tour de force is evident, it pales in comparison to what we see in the Letter to Philemon, where Paul even trots out that he is an old man in chains and that Onesimus is his very heart and he wants Onesimus back. He even says that he knows Philemon will do even more than Paul asks. And the kicker is that this letter is read not privately by Philemon but before the whole church that meets in his house, and Onesimus, the runaway slave, is one of the ones handing him the letter. Talk about pressure to comply! In 2 Cor. 9, in this case verse 12, Paul will call giving to the collection a *leitourgia*, from which we

6. The recent doctoral dissertation at Asbury by Donald Murray Vasser, "Slaves in the Christian Household," which received the highest honors in 2022, has demonstrated the lexical force of Paul's use of the term *isotēs* to deconstruct inequities here in 2 Corinthians between the rich and the poor, and in Colossians to start deconstructing slavery within the church.

get the word "liturgy." It refers to a public service, and in this case a **religious service**. Roman citizens like Paul were expected to perform such services.

Paul has decided not to send just Titus back to finish the collection in Corinth. He is sending reinforcements, including **the brother who is praised among all the assemblies for his gospel ministry** (8:18). We would love to know who this is. My best guess is Silas, who was appointed by the Jerusalem church to travel with Paul as he shared the decree from James (cf. Acts 15; and note the initial greetings in 1 and 2 Thessalonians), though it could be Apollos or Timothy, both of whom had been to Corinth. We cannot be sure. But it looks like 8:22 is a reference to Timothy, Paul's tried, tested, and true coworker. In any case, it becomes obvious that more supervisors of the funds are needed, as Paul indicates that a large sum of money is being administered for the collection (8:20). No wonder Paul is being so careful about this matter!

About the **brothers** being sent, Paul calls them **apostles of the assemblies**, by which he means missionaries sent out by churches, not those apostles commissioned on an ongoing basis by the heavenly Christ himself, of whom Paul says he is the last one (1 Cor. 15:8–9). These other emissaries are sent as witnesses to confirm the eagerness and proof that the Corinthians were rightly boasted about by Paul in terms of their commitment to the collection and their love for the saints.

Second Corinthians 9:7 is a paraphrase of Prov. 22:8 (LXX), which adds to the Hebrew text that "God blesses a cheerful and giving man."[7] The idea of reaping what one sows (2 Cor. 9:6) was in any case proverbial not just in Jewish wisdom literature (see Job 4:8; Hosea 8:7; Sir. 7:3), as non-Jews likewise used this language in rhetorical discourses to refer to reciprocity or even benefaction (see Aristotle, *Rhetoric* 3.3.4; Cicero, *De oratore* 2.65.261). Second Corinthians 9:8 is interesting because of the use of the term *autarkeia*, which Greek authors took to mean "self-sufficiency" (i.e., not being dependent on anyone for anything), something that Paul does not believe in. Paul believes in God-sufficiency, and here his use of *autarkeia* probably is part of his affirmation of a theology of "enough." It means "reducing what one wants for oneself so that one has enough to share with others and create an interdependence with them."[8]

In 9:9 we have another paraphrase, this time of Ps. 112:9, which in its original context refers to the generosity to the poor shown by the righteous (cf. Amos 5), but here Paul probably applies it to God, the ultimate benefactor. And so not surprisingly in 9:10 we find an echo of Isa. 55:10, about God providing **seed** and **bread**. It is unlikely that 9:11 is primarily about material wealth coming

---

7. See Keener, *1–2 Corinthians*, 213.
8. Garland, *2 Corinthians*, 408.

Money in the Sight of God

Any student of the gospel will know that the Bible has plenty to say about how believers should handle and use resources that they have been blessed with. The most basic principle is enunciated by the psalmist, who reminds us, "The earth is the LORD's and the fullness thereof, the world and all the people who dwell in it" (Ps. 24:1). All things and all persons belong to God because, as the next verse says, God created it all. Now, if one is to take this sort of statement seriously, it means that human beings are *not* owners in this world; they are just stewards of God's property, and this should change the whole way one views property or possessions. One should ask continually, "Lord, what would you have me do with your property?"

God has not blessed us with resources merely to meet our needs or wants or desires. He has blessed us so that we can be a blessing to others, and this is the attitude of gratitude that Paul is trying to inculcate in his converts. Neither the attitude that says, "What's mine is mine, and if I share, I am charitable," nor the attitude that says, "What is yours really belongs to the government or the group," is biblical. The principle found in Acts 2:43–47 and 4:32–37 is that God has bestowed things on individuals and they have some freedom in regard to what they do with them. But the beauty of the church in Acts 2:43–47 is that no one was claiming any exclusive right to property, but rather they were sharing all things in common in order to make sure that no one among the believers went without what was truly needed.

Paul is not an advocate of either modern godless capitalism (where individuals think that they really do own things) or godless communism (where the state is said to own the property). Rather, he is an advocate of being generous with what God has blessed a person with, but clearly he does not want to dig a hole in Corinth just to fill one in Jerusalem. What he wants is equity, an equity produced by sharing within the body of Christ. One of the worst witnesses to the world possible in the church is when there are believers who are actually starving, homeless, can't pay their medical bills, and neither the church nor Christian individuals see any obligation to take care of the problem.[a] Paul here is, of course, concerned with a specific problem, involving a specific collection of funds, and is not enunciating a full theology of stewardship, but a careful study of 2 Cor. 8–9 gives us a glimpse of some of his theological and ethical principles.

George Guthrie helpfully summarizes Paul's points as follows: (1) Christians should be generous to all (9:6), especially taking care of the needs of other Christians (cf. Gal. 6:10: "Do good to all, especially to the household of faith"); (2) Christians should trust the principle of the harvest in regard to sowing and reaping (9:6, 10); (3) Christians should be cheerful givers, not giving out of compulsion (9:7); (4) Christians should trust God to meet their needs, in particular what they need to do God's work (9:8–9); (5) giving produces praise of God (9:11–12); (6) giving is a sign and form of obedience to God (9:13); (7) giving binds together diverse Christian groups (9:14).[b]

a. For a longer exposition on a proper theology of stewardship, see Witherington, *Jesus and Money.*
b. Guthrie, *2 Corinthians*, 462.

the Corinthians' way for being generous in regard to the collection. Much more likely is that Paul has in mind what he said in 1 Cor. 1:5, "By him [Christ Jesus] you were enriched in all speech and all knowledge," since Paul has just mentioned these very traits of the Corinthians (cf. 2 Cor. 8:7). It is in 2 Cor. 9:12 that we have the word *leitourgia*, from which we get the word "liturgy." It is talking about a **religious service**, indeed a priestly service, and so Paul is suggesting to the Corinthians that their funds given to the collection are a sacred obligation, or as he calls it in the next verse, **obedience of your confession of the gospel of Christ**. Paul is not a person who contrasts theology with ethics, or religious services involving worship with "good works." The gospel needs to be believed, confessed, and, yes, obeyed, and part of that obedience involves taking care of the poor, as the Old Testament itself says again and again.

If we wonder how all this emotional harangue and angst turned out, Rom. 15:26–27 suggests it was rhetorically effective, for it tells us that Achaia and Macedonia have made their contributions, which Paul and the legates must take to Jerusalem, with Paul leaving from Cenchreae soon. But sadly, things were not to turn out entirely as Paul planned in various regards, as both Acts and Paul's later letters make clear.

The Privilege of Giving

A large Methodist church, which had several thousand members, had the goal that every church member possible would be visited in their home before stewardship Sunday, when all the pledges of resources for the coming year were collected. This canvassing took place usually in November, before the Christmas season. One member of the visiting team was a lawyer who dressed for success in the courts and drove a fancy car. He appeared to be doing very well financially. One of the persons this lawyer was assigned to visit was an elderly lady, a widow living in a trailer on the edge of town, and living on a fixed income that most likely consisted only of her Social Security check. When the lawyer got to the gravel driveway and looked at her aging trailer with concrete block steps leading up to the door, he began to feel guilty about asking her for money, and he resolved just to visit her, and then add a little bit more to his own pledge to the church.

He knocked on the door, and there was the widow, smartly dressed, having cleaned her house and made Toll House cookies and a pitcher of sweet tea. The lawyer was made to feel very welcome. They had a good chat about their church, and then later, as the lawyer was about to stand and leave, the lady said, "Just a minute, I've got my pledge card all filled out and hanging on the refrigerator door," to which the lawyer found himself replying, "Why, that's alright, ma'am, I'll just give a little more, since you clearly live frugally on a fixed income."

Before he could properly finish his sentence, the little woman came right up to him, pointed a finger at his face, and said, "Don't you take away from me the privilege of giving to the cause of Christ." And she turned, got her pledge card, and handed it to the young lawyer, who was by now embarrassed and quietly slipped sheepishly out the door. This woman was much like the widow in the story about Jesus sitting at the temple treasury (Mark 12:41–44; Luke 21:1–4), or in this case about the Achaians and Macedonians who gave very sacrificially. Yes, asking people for money is always a delicate or touchy subject, but no one should ever be ashamed to ask people to give to the cause of the gospel. Or as my bishop once said to our ministers at an annual conference, "You do not need to protect your congregation's wallets for them. They are truly capable of doing that themselves." Amen to that. Paul was not afraid to ask for resources for others. Neither should we be.

Argument Three, Part One

Dueling Ministries

^{10:1}But I myself, Paul, appeal to you by means of [the example of] the meekness and gentleness of Christ, I who am humble among you face-to-face, but bold toward you when away. ²I request that when I am present, I will not need to be bold, with the confidence by which I plan to challenge certain people thinking that we are behaving according to the flesh. ³For although we live in the flesh, we do not wage war according to the flesh, ⁴since the weapons of our warfare are not fleshly but powerful through God for the demolition of strongholds. ⁵We demolish arguments/sophistries, and every "high thing" raised up against the knowledge of God, and we take captive every thought to make it obedient to Christ. ⁶And we are ready to punish any disobedience when your obedience is finished. ⁷Look at what is right before your eyes. If anyone is persuaded that he belongs to Christ, let him remind himself of this: just as he belongs to Christ, so do we! ⁸For if I boast a bit too much about our authority that the Lord gave for building you up, not for tearing you down, I will not be put to shame, ⁹so that I don't want to seem to be terrifying you with my letters, ¹⁰for it is said, "His letters are weighty and powerful but his bodily presence is weak, and his speaking is despicable." ¹¹Let such a person consider this: what we are in our letters when away, we will also be in our actions when present.

¹²For we don't dare classify or compare ourselves with some who commend themselves. But in measuring themselves by themselves and

comparing themselves to themselves, they lack understanding. [13]We, however, will not boast beyond measure, but according to the measure of the standard by which God measures, which reaches as far as you, [14]for we are not overextending ourselves as if we had not reached you, since we have come to you with the gospel of Christ. [15]We are not boasting beyond measure about other people's labors, but have the hope that as your faith increases, our area of ministry among you will be greatly enlarged, [16]so we may preach the gospel to the regions beyond you, without boasting about what has already been done in someone else's area of ministry. [17]So, "Let the one who boasts, boast in the Lord," [18]for it is not the one that commends himself who is approved, but the one the Lord commends.

It is admittedly an odd juxtaposition. Paul begins this argument referring to **the meekness and gentleness of Christ**, and in the same breath he speaks of his intent to be **bold** to **challenge certain people** in Corinth who are behaving in ungodly ways. But clearly the emphatic opening phrase, **I myself, Paul**, makes evident that what he is about to say needs to be emphasized. One wonders what Paul knew about how Jesus was and how he operated. Certainly Jesus was meek and gentle in some ways (e.g., "Take my yoke upon you and learn from me, for I am gentle and humble of heart, and you will find rest for your souls" [Matt. 11:29]), but he was not always this way, and not with everyone. We may conclude that this was Jesus' and Paul's preferred way of relating to people who became their disciples. But that was not always possible. The Corinthians seem to have not preferred this leadership style or approach.

One of the things we must get used to is the fact that Paul lived in a world and culture different from ours. He lived in an honor-and-shame culture where not only was it acceptable to brag or boast; it was expected in order to publicly establish one's honor and sometimes also put others to shame. There are honor columns all over the Greco-Roman world that read like unfettered boasting to a modern Christian, not reflecting humility at all.

But then humility was not seen as a virtue in that pagan world. Indeed, the word "humility" normally was applied to slaves, meaning "servile" or even "base-minded," applied to the proper behavior of slaves in relationship to masters. Humility was not something that a free person would want to emulate if they were a proud Greek or Roman. It is all the more startling, then, to read Phil. 2:5–11 and hear that the Son of God humbled himself and took on the form and very nature of a slave, a servant among human beings. One wonders what the Philippians thought when they first heard this; and then to top that Paul says, "Go and be like that. Go and have this same mind in yourself that was in

Erastus Stone, Corinth

Christ when he did that." Suddenly, humbling oneself became a virtue. If you go to Ephesus and stand in front of the Library of Celsus, you will see four statues of the virtues: Sophia, Arete, Episteme, and Ennoia—in other words, wisdom, excellence, philosophical knowledge, careful thought. There is no statue for humility.

In order to establish one's honor and to be elected to a public office, one might take on a public works project, a "liturgy." And this is exactly what Erastus, a person whom Paul later converted to Christ (Rom. 16:23), did in order to become the city treasurer in Corinth. Just below the theater in Corinth can be found this plaque in the ground: "Erastus, for the office of aedile, paved this plaza at his own expense." We might call that bribery. They called it politics, and playing the honor game, as usual. As has been said, the past is indeed like a foreign country; they do things differently there. So how did Paul's Christian faith change the way he did boasting, the way he viewed establishing honor and avoiding shame?

Two things can be mentioned as we work through the three parts of this final major argument: (1) Paul says that one should, in the main, **boast in the Lord**, especially in regard to conversions or changing lives, for that is the work of God. (2) If one is going to boast about one's own accomplishments, there was a way to do inoffensive self-praise, according to Plutarch's treatise entitled "On Praising Oneself Inoffensively" (*De laude ipsius* 15; *Moralia* 544D). And Cicero, when expositing on this practice, says, "We shall win goodwill for ourselves if we refer to our own [honorable] acts and service without arrogance, if we weaken the effect of the charges brought against or some suspicion of less honorable dealing that has been cast on us, if we talk about the misfortunes that have come to us or the difficulties we still face, and if we use prayers and entreaties with a humble and submissive spirit" (*De inventione rhetorica* 1.16.22).

This is exactly what Paul is doing in 2 Cor. 10–13, *except* that he will boast at length about dishonorable things that the pagan would never normally boast about: all kinds of suffering, being thrown in jail, being beaten multiple times, and all sorts of unfortunate circumstances. Paul focuses on these things because he wants his audience to understand how many trials and difficulties he has gone through and sacrifices he has made *on their behalf.* The goal is to create pathos and a positive feeling in the audience for their apostle. Paul will also resort to irony and some sarcasm when he gets to the point of talking about "visions and revelations" (12:1). In fact, irony marks all of these final chapters of this discourse.[1] Again, all of this sort of discourse was perfectly acceptable in Paul's world. In our world this might well be seen as self-centered preening and self-promotion. But note that Paul's boasting is in the Lord, and it involves inverted self-praise, boasting about things that in the pagan world would be seen as shameful.

One other aspect of Paul's world needs to be taken into account. The culture in the Greek world is called an "agonistic" culture. This means that there was a lot of competition because everything was seen as a zero-sum game: "If you have it, then I don't have it, and if I want it, I have to take it from you in some sort of contest or struggle." There was never a surplus of honor or glory to go around, in the pagan way of thinking. There could only be one ultimate winner. And in good rhetorical practice, Paul has saved the real bone of contention, the major problem he needs to deal with before he arrives, until this final major argument, just as Demosthenes had done before him (*Epistles* 2.26).

It was regular practice not to name your rivals, much less your enemies who were attacking you. Better to condemn them to anonymity and oblivion. Paul never names these **certain people** he refers to. In 10:3–5 we have military language. Paul is preparing for an intellectual battle, and his weapons will not be those used in a fistfight. Paul is preparing, as a good orator would, to demolish flimsy and false arguments, and **sophistries**, things that sound good but are vacuous, having no substance, having no gospel content. In 1 Thess. 5:8, Rom. 13:12, and Eph. 6:10–20 Paul describes the weapons that he will use against the forces of darkness, but here he explains what those weapons are for. N. T. Wright

---

1. See, rightly, Matera, *II Corinthians*, 218.

explains, "They are what you need for the battle against all ideas, arguments, philosophies and world-views that set themselves up against the knowledge of the true God."[2] Paul was all too well aware of all the different religions, cults, philosophies, rituals, and dark arts existing in the empire. There was a lot of competition. Against this, Paul was a profoundly committed monotheist and refused to give way to the religious pluralism of the culture, unlike some Christians then and now.

Unfortunately, many pastors and laypeople have not equipped themselves for the intellectual battles of our age, and as a result the zeitgeist, the spirit of the age, prevails not only outside the church but even within the church, quietly creeping in the back door. One can see this in the horrific battles over issues of human sexuality and marriage in the church, and what is clear is that the church was not and is not very well equipped to fight such battles, and so it simply waves the white flag and surrenders to the cultural drift. Make no mistake, Paul would not have us underestimate the intellectual battle that the church is in, and this means pastors, like Paul, must be trained and able to deconstruct false logic, bad arguments, immoral assumptions—they must **take captive every thought** (10:5). This is a reference to every anti-gospel thought, not just any kind of thought. Paul is not into mind control! Paul does not want his converts to be naive. However smart they may think they are, they can still be led off course by clever arguments posing as "the gospel truth."

And it is precisely these sorts of intellectual battles that Paul does confront in 1–2 Corinthians about matters both theological and ethical, including dealing with the case of a church member who is in an incestuous relationship with his father's wife and who, apparently along with various church members, thinks that this is fine (see 1 Cor. 5:1–5). And sadly, such battles today lead to church splits, massive losses of membership, and an atrocious witness to the world of how the church is capable of being a microcosm of the world rather than a mirror of the truth of the gospel and of the person of Christ.

It raises this question: Do we care enough to follow Paul's lead and confront things raised up against the knowledge of God? Are we brave enough and knowledgeable enough to face rejection with good and fair arguments about the substance of the gospel? Note that Paul's battle in 2 Corinthians is with teachers within the church, not with outsiders. And Paul, unlike some, cares enough to confront those teachers because it matters to the belief system of his converts. It's not about opinions; it's about spiritual realities and living a Christian life. Notice as well that Paul doesn't resort to ad hominem attacks on people. Instead, he's dismantling specious arguments, taking every thought captive for Christ.

---

2. Wright, *Paul for Everyone: 2 Corinthians*, 105.

Paul is working on the contrition of the majority of his audience, and so he says that when he comes, he will deal with the disobedience of **certain people** once the majority has shown their contrition and obedience to the gospel and the apostle's mandates. Paul says that he is prepared to be strong instead of meek in person when he comes, dealing with those causing problems and critiquing Paul. The most interesting verse is where Paul apparently quotes a critique of himself: **for it is said, "His letters are weighty and powerful but his bodily presence is weak, and his speaking is despicable"** (10:10). I like Guthrie's paraphrase: "His letters are intimidating and make a big impression, but he is a pushover in person, and his public speaking is disgraceful."[3] Could this be the opinion of some of Paul's converts, or is this the voice of the outsiders, the pseudo-apostles who have shown up in Corinth after Paul left? We are not sure.[4] In any case, meekness should not be confused with weakness.

Let's consider the essential critique first. Paul likely spoke with an accent, being from the eastern end of the empire and having spent time in Tarsus, Jerusalem, and Antioch; in addition to which, he was a devout Jew who knew Aramaic and Hebrew, and this may also have colored his speech. If Paul is being evaluated on how he sounds, with Attic Greek used as the standard (and remember that the Corinthians are living in the province where Attic Greek was invented and was the normal, time-honored form of Greek), then some would turn up their noses at him. But one suspects that the critique goes deeper, as Paul is being critiqued on the basis of Sophistic rhetoric, mere verbal eloquence, and Paul does not resort to that sort of thing in the first place as he presents the gospel orally.

A further part of the critique is that Paul has an ethos problem. His physical presence is of a man who has been beaten, has scars, and generally appears weak. This is no surprise, considering the affliction catalogs that he has mentioned and will soon list again in 2 Cor. 11–12. But notice as well that the way he comes across in person is said to contrast with the heaviness and force of his letters. Paul's letters were powerful anti-Sophistic rhetoric, and this was recognized.[5]

The problem in part is the Corinthians measuring Paul, and themselves, by other people and not by God's standards of measurement. Paul, as the founding pastor of these Corinthian Christians, believes that he has measured up to God's standard for what he ought to be and do, and so he doesn't believe in measuring himself by other so-called apostles. But clearly, they do measure

3. Guthrie, *2 Corinthians*, 482.
4. There is now a full monograph on who the chief wrongdoer is in 2 Cor. 10–13, and I agree that it is not the same person who was disciplined for sexual immorality in 1 Cor. 5:1–5. See Welborn, *End to Enmity*. The major problem with Welborn's study is that it is based on the probably false conclusion that 2 Cor. 10–13 is likely the aforementioned sorrowful or severe letter.
5. See the discussion in Keener, *1–2 Corinthians*, 218–19.

themselves against Paul, whose letters are heavy but whose ethos is weak and despicable in their view.

Verse 16 is interesting, as it reiterates Paul's basic modus operandi: to boldly go where no apostle or other missionary has gone before and evangelize. He's not making claims about what someone else has done, or claiming someone else's territory or converts. Verse 17 involves a quotation from Jer. 9:24, which is interesting, and the context is important. Leading up to this verse is a long litany of how unfaithful Israel has been, in terms of both idolatry and immorality, and how God is going to judge them, and the women will weep to see the judgment on God's people. Then we hear this: "This is what the Lord says: 'Let not the wise boast of their wisdom or the strong boast of their strength or the rich boast of their riches, but let the one who boasts boast about this: that they have the understanding to know me, that I am the Lord, who exercises kindness, justice and righteousness on earth, for in these I delight,' declares the Lord" (Jer. 9:23–24 NIV). So, this is not just about praising God and boasting in God. The text of Jeremiah says that we should boast that we have the understanding to know God, the Lord of all the earth, who exercises both justice and mercy on the earth. This is not the first time Paul has quoted this text to the Corinthians (see 1 Cor. 1:26–31), and yet the problem of inappropriate boasting persisted in Corinth. But if the Corinthians were eager to hear more boasting, Paul, tongue in cheek, is prepared to give it to them in the second part of this argument—but not at all what they would have expected. Even when we get to 2 Cor. 11, Paul "still brandishes only the power of persuasion based on the truth in Christ."[6]

Sometimes ministers who think that words are not enough to change people and situations resort to strategies and habits learned from secular sources. Stephen Covey's "7 Habits," which have shown up in many church contexts, have some merit to them, but they need to be critically evaluated from a Christian and gospel point of view.[7] One need to ask questions such as these: What counts as success in ministry? More members? A better budget? Or, with Paul, are we more apt to answer, Developing a more spiritually mature congregation? Becoming a more biblically literate leader of God's people? Were Paul to talk about "habits," he would have listed things like regular prayer, self-sacrificial behavior, loving even those whom one finds difficult to get along with. The point is that one cannot simply take over secular habits or strategies and apply them to Christian ministry without critical evaluation and modification.

---

6. Garland, *2 Corinthians*, 426.
7. See, e.g., "The 7 Habits Leader Implementation," FranklinCovey, accessed March 11, 2024, https://www.franklincovey.com/courses/7-habits-leader-implementation/.

Argument Three, Part Two

The Fool's Discourse

^{11:1}I beg you to put up with a little foolishness from me; yes, you must put up with me, ²for I am jealous for you with a godly jealousy, for I have promised you in marriage to one man, to present a pure virgin to Christ. ³But I'm afraid that, as the serpent deceived Eve by his craftiness, your minds may be seduced from a sincere and pure devotion to Christ. ⁴For if someone comes and preaches a Jesus we did not preach, or you receive another spirit that you had not received, or a different gospel that you had not accepted, you put up with it well enough.

⁵For I consider myself in no way inferior to those "super-apostles." ⁶Even if I am not formally trained in rhetoric, that's certainly not the case in knowledge. Indeed, we have in every way made that clear to you in everything. ⁷Or did I commit a sin by humbling myself so you might be exalted, because I preached the gospel to you free of charge? ⁸I looted other assemblies by taking pay from them to minister to you. ⁹When I was present with you and in need, I did not burden any [of you], since the brothers who came from Macedonia supplied my needs. I have kept myself, and will keep myself, from burdening you in any way. ¹⁰As the truth of Christ is in me, this boasting of mine will not be stopped in Achaia. ¹¹Why? Because I don't love you? God knows [I do]. ¹²But I will continue to do what I am doing in order to deny an opportunity to those who want an opportunity to be recognized as our equals in what they boast about. ¹³For such persons are pseudo-apostles,

deceitful workers, disguising themselves as apostles of Christ, [14]and no wonder, since Satan disguises himself as an angel of light. [15]Thus, it is no great surprise that his servants also disguise themselves as servants of righteousness, but their end will be according to their works.

[16]I repeat, let no one think me a fool; but if you do, at least accept me as a fool so that I can also boast a little. [17]What I am saying in this matter of boasting, I am saying not according to the Lord's speaking but according to foolishness. [18]Since many boast according to the flesh, I also will boast. [19]For you, being so wise, gladly put up with fools. [20]In fact, you put up with it if someone enslaves you, if someone preys upon you, if someone takes advantage of you, if someone is arrogant toward you, if someone even slaps you in the face! [21]I confess, to my shame, I was too weak for that! But about whatever anyone dares to boast—I am talking like a fool—I also dare.

[22]Are they Hebrews? So am I. Are they Israelites? So am I. Are they the descendants of Abraham? So am I. [23]Are they servants of Christ? (I'm talking like a crazy person.) I'm a better one, with far more labors, far more imprisonments, with countless floggings, and often near death. [24]Five times I received the thirty-nine lashes from the Jews, [25]three times I was beaten with rods. Once I received a stoning. Three times I was shipwrecked; I have spent a night and a day in the open sea. [26]In my frequent journeys I face dangers from rivers, dangers from thieves, dangers from my own people, dangers from Gentiles, dangers in the city, dangers in the wilderness, dangers at sea, dangers from pseudo-brothers, [27]toil and hardship, many sleepless nights, hunger and thirst, often without food, cold, without clothing. [28]Not to mention other things, there is the daily pressure on me: my concern for all the assemblies. [29]Who is weak, and I am not weak? Who is made to stumble, and I do not burn? [30]If boasting is necessary, I will boast about my weaknesses. [31]The God and Father of the Lord Jesus, who is blessed forever, knows that I am not lying. [32]In Damascus, an ethnarch under King Aretas guarded the city of Damascus in order to arrest me, [33]so I was let down in a basket through a window in the wall and escaped from his hands.

[12:1]Boasting is necessary. It is not profitable, but I will move on to visions and revelations of the Lord. [2]I know a person in Christ who was caught up into the third heaven fourteen years ago. Whether he was in the body or out of the body, I don't know. Only God knows. [3]I know that this man, whether in the body or out of the body—I don't know, only God knows—[4]was caught up into Paradise and heard inexpressible words that a human being is not allowed to speak. ⁵I will boast about this person, but not about myself except of my weaknesses. ⁶For if I wish to boast, I wouldn't be a fool, because I would be telling the truth. But I will spare you, so that no one will evaluate me with something beyond what he sees in me or hears from me, ⁷especially because of the extraordinary revelations. Therefore, so that I would not exalt myself, a thorn in the flesh was given to me, an angel of Satan to torment me so that I would not exalt myself. ⁸About this I pleaded with the Lord three times in order that it would leave me, ⁹but he said to me, "My grace is sufficient for you, for my power is completed/perfected in weakness." Therefore, I will most gladly boast all the more about my weaknesses, so that residing upon me is the power of Christ. ¹⁰So, I take pleasure in weaknesses, insults, hardships, persecutions, and in difficulties for the sake of Christ, for when I am weak, then I am strong.

This part of the third, and last, major argument in this discourse is full of irony, invective, sarcasm (**I confess, to my shame, I was too weak for that**), tongue-in-cheek critiques, and more. And here again we need to remind ourselves that what is persuasive in one culture may be repulsive in another, and in any case, none of us, including even church planters today, have the same apostolic authority or Scripture-creating inspiration that Paul did, even if from time to time we have prophetic words from God or share regularly our spiritual gifts in worship. So, this sort of material must be studied in its original context and used prayerfully and carefully today in order to make sure that it is a word on target.

For example, preaching or teaching on Paul's thorn in the flesh could lead to some good reflections on what to do when God's answer to prayer is, "No, I'm not removing that problem from your life, because I can use it to make you a more powerful and effective witness for me. My power is made perfect in your weakness; my grace is sufficient for you" (cf. 4:7–12; 6:3–10).[1]

The very first segment of this portion of Paul's argument brings into play two interesting analogies: the assemblies in Corinth are likened to a bride, betrothed to Christ (see also Eph. 5:21–33); and at the same time an analogy is drawn with the story of Eve and her beguiling by the serpent (2 Cor. 11:2–3). In this drama, the false teachers, or pseudo-apostles, are the beguilers, Paul is the father of the bride who arranged the marriage, and the Corinthians, while being a new creation, are also young Christians who are naive and can be led astray.

1. On Paul sharing the sufferings of Christ, see the discussion in Wright, *Paul for Everyone: 2 Corinthians*, 123.

Paul doesn't want his offspring to be a runaway bride![2] In the Old Testament the bride imagery appears when Israel has shown a lack of covenant faithfulness (Isa. 54:6–7; Jer. 2:2; 3:6; Ezek. 23:5–8; Hosea 1:1–2:2). And notice that the wedding is still in the future, much like the image in Rev. 21:2. Paul does not believe that the relationship between God and his people has been "consummated" yet. The bride could still run away or become unfaithful. In fact, that is precisely what Paul warns against when he speaks about the church being like Eve, subject to being deceived, in this case by the serpent of false teachers with their false gospel. All this is by way of saying that Paul is concerned about the real possibility of his converts committing apostasy. He doesn't think that their relationship with Christ is a done deal. They are only betrothed to Christ and are not yet his bride, sharing a permanent union with him. Paul, as the spiritual father of the bride, is trying to protect and guard his converts from defection so that they can be presented at the second coming to Christ as a virgin who has not been unfaithful, who has not been seduced away from pure devotion to Christ, the Spirit, the real gospel.

The next part of the text sounds a bit like Gal. 1:6–9, where Paul speaks about "another [*allos*] gospel," which in the Greek means not merely a "second gospel" but rather an "alternative gospel." Here in Gal. 1, *allos* (v. 7) seems to be used as a synonym for *heteros* (v. 6), but in both cases the idea is a **different** one—a different Jesus, a different spirit, and a different gospel. But Paul knows that there is no other real Jesus, real Spirit, real gospel. There is the reality, and everything else is a false parody. Paul doesn't want his converts to fall for buying the cheap knockoffs when they already have the genuine gospel, the real Lord and Spirit. Here again the content of the message matters, not merely the attractive packaging of the product, but unfortunately, Paul does not explain in any detail what is entailed in the false teachers' "other" gospel, or different Jesus. Overall, it appears that he means that the crucified Christ whom Paul was preaching was not the Jesus whom the false teachers advocated. As Gal. 1:6–9 makes evident, Paul is prepared to be dogmatic about this sort of matter. Doctrine matters; theological substance should not be a matter of indifference.

Unfortunately, the United States and other countries, especially Western ones, have often suffered from the preaching and teaching of a false gospel and of a pale shadow of the real Jesus and the real Spirit. H. Richard Niebuhr, rightly critiquing liberal Protestantism, complained that the message was so watered down that it became this: "A God without wrath brought men without sin into a Kingdom without judgment through the ministrations of a Christ without

---

2. See the discussion in Wright, *Paul for Everyone: 2 Corinthians*, 112–16.

a Cross."[3] And one could add: everyone is going to heaven regardless of the content of one's belief, since there is no hell.

We do not know the full nature of the pseudo-apostles' reframing of the gospel, but given how much Paul emphasizes mock boasting, and his suffering, and given how much he emphasizes the message "Christ and him crucified" even as early as 1 Cor. 1–4, and the suffering that is involved in allegiance to Christ for his messengers, suffering is probably a main part of the problem with the false teachers' message—rather like the modern false gospel that says, "If you just have enough real faith, you will not have to suffer, you will stay in good health, and God will bless you with riches beyond your wildest dreams."

Paul's statement in 2 Cor. 11:6 is interesting. He refers to himself, in regard to his public speaking, as an *idiōtēs*. This does not mean an illiterate person, nor does it mean an unskilled person; it means a person who may not have received formal, higher-level training in some aspect of rhetoric beyond the *progymnasmata* (preliminary rhetorical exercises). But it is also perfectly possible that Paul is speaking tongue in cheek: "Even if I am an *idiōtēs* in speaking, I am not one in knowledge." This is a conditional sentence (a present-tense real condition), but the Greek sentence doesn't even have verbs; they are implied. The point in any case is that Paul is superior to his rivals in regard to knowing and sharing the content of the gospel, even if his rhetorical *delivery* of the message is not at a professional level.

Murray Harris puts it this way: "But although technically a 'non-professional,' an [*idiōtēs*] could be knowledgeable in a particular field. The term 'does not rule out the individual's informal acquaintance with a subject or practice in it.' . . . [Paul] is not denying that he has any knowledge of rhetoric. . . . If, as we have suggested, [*ho logos*] in 10:10 refers to Paul's speaking ability, including adroitness in extempore speech, it is likely that [*tō logō*] [in 11:6] has a similar reference, 'public speaking.'"[4] I would point out that this is likely about how Paul orally *delivered* the rhetoric, and in an oral culture effective delivery was a crucial part of persuasion. So, Paul's rhetorically adept letters are to be contrasted not so much with his message in person but with how he delivered the message, having no professional training in that regard.

But there may be something else going on in this verse. Dio Chrysostom, roughly a contemporary of Paul, contrasts himself with the Sophists by claiming he is "unskilled" or an amateur in rhetoric compared to the Sophists (*Orations* 12.15); he even calls himself an *idiōtēs* compared to the Sophists

3. This is from Niebuhr's classic book *The Kingdom of God in America*. This book originally came out in 1937.
4. Harris, *Second Epistle to the Corinthians*, 748–49. In the middle of that sentence Harris is quoting Kennedy, *New Testament Interpretation*, 95.

(*Orations* 42.3). Now, Dio Chrysostom was a well-trained rhetorician and a famous orator. So, when he says this, he is being ironic. In view of how much of Paul's discourse here involves irony, he likely is being ironic in 11:6 in the same way as Dio Chrysostom, merely contrasting himself with the Sophistic verbal eloquence of his opponents in Corinth.[5] Consider just how much Paul sounds like Dio Chrysostom in the following ironic excerpt from one of the latter's speeches:

> Gentlemen, I have come before you not to display my talents as a speaker nor because I want money from you, or expect your praise. For I know not only that I myself am not sufficiently well equipped to satisfy you by my eloquence, but also that your circumstances are not such as to need my message. Furthermore, the disparity between what you demand of a speaker and my own powers is very great. For it is my nature to talk quite simply and unaffectedly and in a manner in no wise better than that of any ordinary person; whereas you are devoted to oratory to a degree that is remarkable, I may even say excessive, and you tolerate as speakers only those who are very clever. Nay, my purpose in coming forward is not to gain your admiration—for I could not gain that from *you* even were I to utter words more truthful than those of the Sibyl or of Bacis—but rather that no one may look askance at me or ask others who I am and whence I came. For at present quite possibly people suspect that I am one of your wiseacres, one of your know-it-alls. (*Orations* 35.1–2)[6]

In 11:7–8 Paul returns to the previous sore spot: his refusal of patronage from any Corinthian believer. It is interesting that almost never does Paul use "sin" in the singular to refer to a particular sin, as he does here (the only other place is Rom. 4:8). Normally, "sin" in the singular refers not to a particular sin but to sin in general as some sort of evil power in the life of the individual or of the world. And here again, the accusation is false, and so the reference has an ironic tone.[7] Paul says sarcastically that he **looted**, or "pillaged" or "extorted," the Macedonians for financial support. He is, of course, deliberately exaggerating, as becomes clear from reading both 2 Cor. 8–9 and the Letter to the Philippians. No, Paul had a parity relationship with the Philippians, a relationship of "giving and receiving," as it was called, which did not involve patronage.

5. But see a different view in Oropeza, *Exploring Second Corinthians*, 605.
6. Author's translation. This is why my longtime friend Bruce Winter has made the suggestion that the term *idiōtēs* as in the quote just cited refers to a person who is trained in rhetoric but who chooses not to function as some place's or some person's public orator or teacher of rhetoric. See Winter, *Philo and Paul among the Sophists*, 224–25. In any case, Paul eschews mere verbal pyrotechnics and eloquence for their own sakes in the attempt to persuade an audience. He is no Sophist.
7. See Guthrie, *2 Corinthians*, 519.

So generous were the Philippians, even when they were poor, that Paul toward the end of the letter has to tell them that they can stop giving and giving and giving. At that point in the early 60s, while Paul was under house arrest in Rome, locals like Priscilla and Aquila or Andronicus and Junia (see Rom. 16:1–16) probably were looking after the apostle. Another euphemistic technical phrase about money is "sending me on my way," which Paul uses in Rom. 15 (vv. 24, 28), speaking about the Roman Christians providing him with supplies and funds to get him to his next destination, and in this case, he was hoping to go to Spain. This sort of technical phrase we also find in 3 John 6.

Money was always a delicate matter, and Paul had to use discernment as to when to receive support and when not. It depended on whether strings were attached to the money or whether it did not involve entangling alliances. In any case, Paul wanted to share the gospel free of charge. What we also learn from all of this is that Paul did *not* always provide his own support by leatherworking, and he did not have a principle that missionaries should always do that. Indeed, his principle was "A workman is worthy of his hire" (see 1 Tim. 5:18), and so he had a right to receive pay for his ministry, and he also had the right to refuse to be paid. Manual labor was looked down on by a good deal of the Greco-Roman elite, and working with animal hides, from a Jewish point of view, could make a person unclean. And when one adds to this that Paul did it to avoid patronage in Corinth, it was problematic for many.

The modern "tentmaking" mission paradigm needs to be changed to actually comport with what Paul says. The implication of 2 Cor. 11:9–10 seems to be that some Corinthians thought Paul's not receiving patronage was a sign that he didn't really love them. Paul swears an oath that God knows that Paul does indeed love the Corinthians (v. 11). But in fact, Paul turns the tables by suggesting that the false teachers are not his equals, because he offered the gospel free of charge. Not so these false teachers. Paul directly calls a spade a spade in verse 13: **Such persons are pseudo-apostles, deceitful workers, disguising themselves as apostles of Christ**. Deception and disguise are the modus operandi of Satan and the serpent, so Paul is painting these persons with a satanic brush. But let's be clear that this is not mere hyperbole or polemics. Paul really thinks that his converts are in spiritual danger from these **pseudo-apostles** (a term that Paul seems to have coined himself). Paul foresees that their fate will accord with their false teaching and actions.

It is in the fool's discourse, or lament, that Paul really ratchets up the irony and sarcasm, beginning at 11:16. Paul prefaces the whole thing with the disclaimer that he is deliberately speaking in a foolish way (not in the way he would normally speak under the Lord's guidance), and the whole point is to shame not just his audience in general but their embracing of the false teachers. So, he will boast about things that the pseudo-apostles would never think to boast about. Notice the sarcasm in verse 19: the Corinthians **gladly put up with fools** and worldly boasting because they are **so wise** (cf. 1 Cor. 3:18–20; 4:10; 6:5; 8:1–7; 13:2)! Verse 20 indicates that these opponents have been gobbling up the Corinthians' resources, enslaving them, and even abusing them.

Finally, at 11:22, we begin to get a picture of who these pseudo-apostles are. Clearly, they are Jews, and apparently not diaspora ones, as they are **Hebrews**, which in this case would mean those who can speak Hebrew (and Aramaic). Apparently they brag about their lineage from Abraham, as true Israelites. But these are not non-Christian Jews; these are people claiming to be servants of Jesus Christ, about which Paul says, "Even if they are, I am more so!" (v. 23). Notice that Paul says nothing about the pseudo-apostles trying to impose circumcision, Sabbath, or food laws on the Corinthians; rather, they brag about their charismatic experiences and gifts. These men are not likely either the Judaizers who bothered Paul's Galatian converts or the men who came from James to Antioch (see Gal. 2:11–14). We do not know where they came from.

But then Paul turns to criteria for boasting, which he alone can claim. He's worked harder (for the Corinthians), been in prison more frequently, been whipped more often, and the tale of woe goes on and on (11:23–27). And the point of all this is the cumulative effect. One may doubt that pseudo-apostles have ever been in jail or whipped, never mind received death threats, or been in all sorts of perilous circumstances. The point of the long litany of woe is not only to silence the boasting of the opposition but also to stop his audience from being enamored with the false teachers. We may well ask, When had all this happened to Paul? He's writing only after his second missionary journey, in the mid- to late 50s, and the first missionary journey was only in the late 40s, before the Jerusalem conference in about AD 50. When was he shipwrecked multiple times? We don't know. This long list does not correspond in detail to the summary accounts in Acts. But we may be sure that these things really did happen to Paul the apostle of Christ at some point—some of them perhaps during his years after conversion and after the first visit to Jerusalem when he went back to his home province of Syria-Cilicia, some of them perhaps when he was in Arabia immediately after conversion. We can't say more about that.

Here I make a few comments about Paul saying, **Five times I received the thirty-nine lashes**. This punishment is referred to in Deut. 25:2–3 ("not . . . more than forty lashes") and was reserved for some severe offense committed in a Jewish meeting, in this case in a synagogue. Josephus says that the punishment was adjusted to thirty-nine (*Jewish Antiquities* 4.238, 248), perhaps to avoid miscounting and thus going beyond what the law said. The punishment was administered with a leather strap. What this tells us about Paul is that he continued to go and share the gospel in synagogues, even after having been beaten in this way multiple times. This is because, as he says in Rom. 1:16, the gospel is for the Jew first, and we see this Pauline practice of going to the synagogue first as a repeated pattern in Acts.

This sort of beating could sometimes lead to death, which says something about Paul's strength and stamina, but it is also possible that Paul was all too familiar with this punishment because he administered it to Christians when he was a Pharisaic zealot, dragging people off to be judged by the Sanhedrin. What this suggests from the synagogue side of things is that Paul was seen, at a minimum, as a deceiver, a wayward brother, the very sort of thing that Paul is now accusing his opponents of. If Paul had simply been seen as apostate, Frank Matera suggests, he would have been expelled from the synagogue.[8] However, Paul was a traveling apostle. He was not a regular member of any of the synagogues that he visited during his missionary work. And the accounts in Acts suggest that sometimes he was expelled from synagogues, even after only one or two visits. Further, Paul also mentions in this same litany of woe that he had been stoned (11:25; cf. Deut. 17:5–7; 22:22–24, a punishment for apostasy). So, I am doubtful that the thirty-nine lashes indicates that those administering it simply or always thought of Paul as a wayward Jew who needed correction. That's not what the combination of whipping and stoning suggests.

What Paul says in 11:28–29 is important. He was not going through all those trials and tribulations for nothing; he was doing it for his converts and potential new converts. Paul felt it viscerally when things went wrong with his assemblies. And he got very upset when some of them were led away into sin by false teachers, servants of the serpent (see 11:13–15). Notice that Paul speaks of anxiety about all the churches. By the time Paul wrote 2 Corinthians he had churches in Galatia, Asia, Bithynia, Macedonia, and Achaia. That's a lot to be anxious about. Sometimes ministers of a single church think they have it rough, but when they read these Pauline accounts, they realize that they actually have it much better than the apostle Paul did and have much less to be anxious about. In verses 30–31 Paul swears another oath combined with a doxology (cf. 1:23; 11:10–11).

Verse 32 is fascinating, as it provides us with a window into Paul's hidden years (cf. Acts 9:23–25). King Aretas IV was the ruler of Nabatea, a kingdom in modern-day Jordan, whose capital was Petra. This is probably where Paul went immediately after his experience on the Damascus road.[9] He must have stirred up some trouble while he was in Arabia, because the king's ethnarch, his

---

8. Matera, *II Corinthians*, 267.
9. See Witherington and Myers, *Paul of Arabia*, a historical-fiction volume done with my former doctoral student Jason Myers.

representative in Damascus, was under orders to capture Paul and send him back to Petra. Paul was a wanted man. There is perhaps some evidence that the Nabatean kingdom had stretched far enough north to include Damascus itself at this point. What we know for sure is that after King Herod Antipas ditched his first wife, who was the daughter of Aretas, in order to marry Herodias, the wife of his brother, Aretas went on the warpath and conquered some of the territory of Herod east of the Jordan in AD 36. The Nabatean kingdom was a kingdom expanding, and importantly it was not yet a part of the Roman Empire. This did not occur until AD 106, after Aretas IV's reign, when the Romans took control and called the territory Arabia Petraea.

In any case, Paul tells a joke on himself that the Roman Corinthians would get. In Roman warfare, a soldier got an award, a so-called wall crown, for being first up the wall into a city that was being besieged. N. T. Wright describes this as follows:

> In the world of ancient Rome, where military might and bravery was regarded as one of the highest of the virtues, . . . was the award known as the *corona muralis*, or "crown of the wall." It was a literal crown, made to look like the wall of a city, complete with gates and battlements. A marble statue of the goddess *Tyche* ("Lady Luck"), dating to the generation or so after Paul, has been found by archaeologists in Corinth, wearing one of these crowns. . . .
>
> The *corona muralis* was awarded, and had been for many centuries by Paul's day, for one military achievement in particular. . . . [It] was awarded to the soldier who, during the siege, *was the first one over the wall.*[10]

As Wright goes on to relate, often this crown was awarded posthumously because usually the first one over the wall was killed during the assault. And because of this, people were skeptical if a Roman soldier came home from a battlefield claiming that he had done this. "So in order to claim 'the crown of the wall,' the person who actually was the first over the wall had to return to Rome and swear a solemn oath, invoking the gods to witness that he was telling the truth. 'I swear before the holy gods, who know I am telling the truth, that, when we were attacking the city, I was the first one over the wall.' And [only then] would the crown be awarded."[11] By dramatic contrast, Paul brags that he was first *down* the wall in a basket (vv. 32–33). I like to call this "Paul the basket case," but in any case, it's a humorous example of inverted self-praise.[12] Notice that this precedes the discussion of Paul's uplifting revelations, juxtaposed nicely with

---

10. Wright, *Paul for Everyone: 2 Corinthians*, 125–26.
11. Wright, *Paul for Everyone: 2 Corinthians*, 126.
12. On this, see Witherington, *Conflict and Community*, 444.

this "down" lifting, humiliating exit from Damascus.[13] Like that soldier claiming the crown, Paul has just sworn an oath that God knows he is not lying (v. 31).

Paul lists this down-the-wall "achievement" last, as if it is his *crowning* achievement, his greatest triumph in the realm of inverted self-praise. And of course, once Paul was down the wall, he ran away from the ethnarch of Aretas. Like Christ's crucifixion, this looked like defeat. Instead, Christ rose again from the dead and commissioned people like Paul. And as for Paul, he lived to further fight the battle for the gospel after escaping Damascus, though ultimately, he too would be martyred, not in Jerusalem but in Rome.

Paul is boasting about all the wrong things in order to shame the audience for being impressed with the claims of the pseudo-apostles and the usual things that they themselves bragged about when talking about personal achievements. He puts on the mask of the "fool" who boasts according to human standards and not according to the Lord's standards, not to entertain his audience but to make them see themselves as they are. Temporarily, and sarcastically, Paul appears to brag like his opponents do. The whole point is that since the death and resurrection of Christ, they were all living in an upside-down world when it came to honor and shame. What would have been seen as shameful, suffering—in particular, suffering a humiliating death on a cross—was now the greatest event that ever happened in human history, with God's Son dying for the sins of the world. And so, Christ's apostle likewise touts things that no one would tout, things that would be considered humiliating defeats, like the basket story. Paul is indeed in the business of changing the values of his culture, and in some cases turning them upside down. When the least, the last, and the lost become the most, the first, and the found in a gospel reversal foreshadowing the kingdom conditions, things indeed would seem to be upside down to many pagans, and not a few Jews as well.

Michael Card, a Christian musician, wrote some apt lyrics about 1 Cor. 1:20–25 that are just as suitable here:

> When we in our weakness believed we were strong,
> He became helpless to show we were wrong.[14]

At the beginning of 2 Cor. 12, Paul is likely talking about himself in the third person, but this passage is definitely one of the most debated in all Pauline literature, and precisely because it is part of the fool's speech, it is hard to know exactly how to evaluate it. Is he talking about himself or someone else

---

13. See Keener, *1–2 Corinthians*, 237.
14. Michael Card, "God's Own Fool," track 9 on *Scandalon*, SPR 1117 (Sparrow, 1985). Thank you to George Guthrie for pointing me to this reference.

having a vision? Is he bragging or just shaming his opponents' grandiose claims about visions and revelations? In light of both Paul's previous **boasting** about himself and his reference here to having a **thorn in the flesh** that keeps him from becoming overly elated about his visionary experiences, the context surely indicates that this account is about Paul himself—but why in the third person? As it turns out, it was a proper rhetorical device to talk about oneself in the third person as a more modest way to speak about one's experiences.[15] After all, Christ, the one Paul modeled himself on, regularly spoke of himself in the third person as "the Son of Man."

It is interesting that Paul picks a vision from **fourteen years** prior, which would likely put it in his period of being in Syria-Cilicia before Barnabas came and brought him to Antioch. And again, it is a tongue-in-cheek kind of boasting meant to counter the claims of the pseudo-apostles about their visions and revelations. The hilarious part is that Paul says that this person was **caught up** to the highest level of **heaven, Paradise** (cf. Luke 23:43; 2 En. 8:1; Apoc. Mos. 37:5; 40:1; and on there being three levels to heaven, T. Levi 2–3). He says that he heard there **inexpressible** things that no one is permitted to tell. What a tease! Doubtless the false teachers were bragging about things they had heard and could relate from their visions.

And notice, Paul says absolutely nothing about seeing anything! What kind of visionary says that he has visions, and then just speaks about something he heard that he is not permitted to share? Possibly we should relate this to Paul's admission just after this that he has a **thorn in** his **flesh**, and my best guess is that the **thorn** has to do with his sight. In Gal. 4:13–15 Paul says that the Galatians would have plucked out their own eyes and given them to Paul because he came to them with some obvious infirmity. This cannot be a random comment. I'm thinking Paul had some vision issues that continued to plague him throughout his ministry. And this could explain his ethos problem as well. The eyes were viewed by the ancients as the windows on the soul, and furthermore, they believed that the eyes are projectors of light or darkness, hence the "evil eye" convention.

If Paul had eye problems when he came to the Corinthians, what kind of positive visionary could he have been? Had Paul's opponent suggested that his physical appearance was what was despicable and weak? Some additional evidence that could support this theory is that Paul says at the end of Galatians that he writes with large letters (6:11), like a person who needs a large-print edition of a book. We also know that he used scribes to write down his letters

---

15. For a helpful, detailed, and convincing defense that Paul is talking about himself as a visionary here, see Thrall, *Second Epistle to the Corinthians*, 2:772–832.

What about Speaking in Tongues?

It has been said that you become what you admire, and one of the professors I met when I began my seminary education was Gordon Fee, an Assemblies of God minister and first-class New Testament scholar, whose energetic and fervent lectures were exciting and inspiring, especially when he taught Acts or 1 Corinthians or Revelation. The girl I was dating at the time was my next-door neighbor, Ann Sears, a high school biology teacher, who had gone through sixteen years of parochial Catholic education, and like her, I had never encountered up close a real Pentecostal person who not only affirmed spiritual gifts such as speaking in tongues and prophecy but spoke in tongues himself.

We encountered this when we began to attend Gordon Fee's in-home Bible study, which turned out to be unlike any Bible study I had ever been a part of before, and I had been part of an InterVarsity fellowship group at the University of North Carolina at Chapel Hill. Speaking in tongues quietly during prayer time was what we heard, and it was moving. Ann was led to commit herself to the Lord in a new way, and she wanted to keep studying the Bible in a way that she had not been encouraged to do before. Ann later became my wife, and we continue to study the Word together.

As for me, I decided to go to a charismatic service at Tremont Temple Baptist Church in Boston for a special service of healing, speaking in tongues, and even exorcisms, led by Derek Prince, a British-educated Bible teacher. There was a point in time when individuals who wanted to receive a spiritual gift such as tongues were invited to come to the altar rail, kneel, have hands laid on them, and pray for the gift. Now, you need to understand that never once as a lifelong Methodist had I ever been to or seen a service like this one. There were even some people rolling in the aisles and foaming at the mouth as they were being exorcised. Whatever else one can say, the atmosphere was heavy with spiritual weight, and it was electrifying. I had never encountered anything like this in the United Methodist Church. Not once. Long story short, I did receive the gift of tongues, but the main thing that this did for me was to draw me closer to the Lord, and it provided confirmation that the Spirit was in my life, guiding me, and that I was on the right path in going to seminary and pursuing further education. It was a powerful confirmation of my calling.

That summer when I went home, I participated in a Bible study with my previous classmates from UNC who lived in Charlotte. They told me about an eight-o'clock morning worship service at Resurrection Lutheran

Church that involved all sorts of exciting things, including singing in tongues, good biblical preaching, personal sharing of testimonies, and the Lord's Supper. And this had been a Missouri Synod Lutheran Church that had a reputation of not being like that at all. God's Spirit was moving in amazing ways across denominational lines. I loved those services, even though they weren't happening at the Methodist churches I attended, and I was fed and grew because of those experiences. The Spirit's gifts are alive and well today as they were two thousand years ago, including gifts like visionary experiences such as Paul had in 2 Cor. 12:1–10.

(Rom. 16:22; cf. 1 Cor. 16:21; Col. 4:18; 2 Thess. 3:17), and yet clearly he is literate. And finally, why in the latter part of his ministry did he need an attending physician, Luke, to travel with him during the third missionary journey and on to Jerusalem and then to Rome? Surely, he was someone who had a chronic but treatable problem that did not prevent him from fulfilling his calling. Why do we hear in the Pastoral Epistles, at the end of Paul's life, "Luke alone is with me"? (2 Tim. 4:11). If you put all this together, it adds up to this: Paul's thorn in the flesh had to do with his eyes. Yes, he recovered some sight after being blinded on the Damascus road, but apparently not entirely, and it continued to bother him. Finally, note that Paul mentions the **thorn** or stake **in the flesh** directly after speaking about his **extraordinary revelations** (12:7). It seems that there must be a connection.

It is a master stroke to use an account of a peak spiritual experience, a vision, as a deflation device for the audience. Now, in the general Greco-Roman culture there was indeed some understanding about the problems of attempting to "fly too high," which is why we have the mythological story about Icarus flying too near the sun, and the wax in his manufactured wings melting, resulting in disaster and death. One can also cite the fact that even at a Roman triumph, where the general or emperor was boldly riding down the road leading his own parade in Rome, having a red-powdered face to make him look like the god of war, Mars, or even Jupiter Optimus Maximus, there was a slave standing beside him in the chariot whispering in his ear, "Remember, you are mortal," not a god. Unfortunately, some of the emperors, from at least Caligula on, did not listen to the voice of warning, and the emperor cult became a growth industry across the Roman Empire. But they were the mere parody of which King Jesus is the reality.

This section of the argument closes with the affirmation that since God's power is made perfect and manifested in Paul's weakness, Paul is perfectly content to delight in his weaknesses and hardships, persecutions, and other dif-

More on Visions and Revelations

It is one thing to talk about personal visions, whether one receives them during the daytime or at night in the form of dreams. The ancients certainly believed that visions could reveal some truths, including truths about the future, as the many references to such things in Greek and Latin and early Jewish literature attest.[a] But a vision is one thing; a prophecy is another; and an apocalyptic prophecy is still a third thing. Sometimes a vision was simply a revelation from a deity to a particular person and not necessarily meant to be passed on as a revelation to others. One suspects that Paul's vision was of that sort, not least because Paul had not previously mentioned it in earlier letters, and here in 2 Cor. 12 he mentions it in a very general sort of way to make a point of shaming his rivals. There were undoubtedly, however, visions that were meant to be conveyed to others as a sort of prophecy, such as we find in Ezek. 1, or Dan. 7, or Zechariah with his night visions, and of course the book of Revelation.

What needs to be stressed about visionary or apocalyptic prophecy is that when it involves heavenly things, or encounters with God, the language suddenly involves analogies (notice how many times in Ezek. 1 we have the phrase "it was like"), metaphors, and poetry and is often highly symbolic in character. The language is meant to be referential, but the description is not by any means literal. Why not? For the very good reason that human language is too limited to describe literally something as enormous or overwhelming as an encounter with God or a seeing into heaven. Purely auditory revelations to a prophet could simply be repeated verbatim, and this is what we find in classical prophecy in the Old Testament, where we find the formula "Thus says Yahweh . . ." and what follows is the prophet repeating what he was told. This became impossible when prophecies involved both an auditory and a visual dimension. Paul may have had numerous visions and revelations from God, like the one described in Acts 9:1–19; 22:6–16; 26:12–18, but the passage in 2 Cor. 12:1–10 suggests that they were infrequent, or else why dredge up a reference to something that happened fourteen years prior? In any case, it is clear enough that Paul envisioned himself as a prophet as well as an apostle, and as such he claimed to have some direct revelations from God in Christ in the form of visions.

a. Homer, *Iliad* 1.63; 5.150; Xenophon, *Anabasis* 3.1.11; 4.3.8; 6.1.22; *De equitum magistro* 9.9; Pausanias, *Graeciae descriptio* 4.19.5–6; 9.26.4; Longus, *Daphnis and Chloe* 1.7; 2.23, 26–27; 3.27; 4.35; Appian, *Historia romana* 11.9.56; 12.12.83; Quintus Curtius, *Historiae Alexandri Magni* 4.2.17; Arrian, *Anabasis Alexandri* 2.18.1; Babrius, *Fables* 136.3–4; Achilles Tatius, *Leucippe and Cleitophon* 1.3.2; 4.1.4; 7.12.4; Chariton, *Chaereas and Callirhoe* 1.12.5; 2.9.6; 3.7.4; 4.1.2; 5.5.5–7; 6.2.2; 6.8.3; cf. *Orphic Hymns* 85–87; Epidauros inscriptions; Tacitus, *Annals* 2.14; Marcus Aurelius, *Meditations* 1.17.8; cf. Virgil, *Aeneid* 4.556–57; 7.415–20; Ovid, *Metamorphoses* 9.685–701; 15.653–54; Ezekiel the Tragedian 68–89; Sibylline Oracles 3.293; Philo, *On the Migration of Abraham* 190. Many thanks to Craig Keener for this list of references.

ficulties because when he is weak, and yet people's lives are changed, it becomes evident that the real change agent is Christ; the all-surpassing power and grace come from him and through Paul, not from Paul himself.

Something should be said about prayer at this juncture. Paul was, of course, a person who prayed a great deal for many things, and here we are told that he asked God **three times** to remove this thorn or stake in his flesh. God's answer, however, was no! There is so much Christian mythology these days about prayer, and often it is not grounded in what the Bible says about prayer. From this text we certainly should conclude that a devout person, even a visionary person who spoke God's very Word that changed lives, could be told no by God in regard to some things. No, then, is an answer to prayer. This means that we need to stop talking about "unanswered" prayers.

God always answers the prayers of his people, but sometimes the answer is not what we would like, or wish, or ask for. Not only is "no" an answer to prayer, but so also is "not now," or "not in this way," or "not with this person." There are many different ways God can answer prayer, and if we ask for something that is definitely against God's will for our life, God will indeed say no.

What, then, is the relationship between faith and prayer? Obviously, praying, however infrequent, is a small indicator of some sort of faith in God or a higher power. While there may be a positive correlation between having some saving faith and an answer to prayer, just as there can be a negative correlation between lack of faith and no positive answer to prayer ("You have not, because you ask not" [cf. James 4:2]), it is simply not possible to pray so fervently that you make God an offer that God can't refuse. Prayer is not a means of twisting the arm of a reluctant deity to act. God is definitely not reluctant to act for his people at the right time, in the right way, for the right ends.

And one can well ask, Why, exactly, do we pray if an all-knowing and all-wise God already knows what we are going to pray? We surely are not informing God about something that God is unaware of. God is not sitting up in heaven saying to the angels, "Wow, did you just hear that prayer from one of our beloved saints? I had never thought about that before!" No, the point of praying is to be in touch with God, to further our own relationship with God, and even to be used by God as a means and messenger of his will being done on earth, in our own lives, and in the lives of others.

While God doesn't have to do it this way, as God could act unilaterally because God loves his people and desires to have a blessed, ongoing relationship with them, he enlists their help in accomplishing his salvific and kingdom purposes. The apostle Paul knows all this, and so he knows that while God always answers the prayers of those who seek him, sometimes the answer must be and will be no. God answers our prayers not always at the point of our request but at the point of our need. In 1 Kings 19 Elijah prayed to die. God instead strengthened him for the journey to Horeb and then recommissioned him to go back to Israel with more coworkers to accomplish God's mission that Elijah had been called to.

And finally, since we sign our prayers "in the name of Jesus," it would be well if we ask ourselves this in advance about the prayer: Is this something that Jesus would pray or would have us pray? If you are going to sign his name to a prayer, surely it ought to conform to the will of Christ. Sometimes it is indeed Christ's will that we suffer for the sake of the gospel. If this can be the case even with Paul himself, why should we expect to be exempt? Some of the greatest saints in all of Christian history suffered greatly for the Lord's sake and even gave up their lives at an early age (cf. Heb. 11:8–38). One cannot tell the state of one's faith from evaluating how much one has suffered in life. Nor is it possible in most cases to correlate sickness or disabilities with sin (see Jesus' answer to his disciples in John 9:1–3 about the blind man's condition). We live in a fallen world, and some of the healthiest people are the worst sinners, and some of the sickest ones are people of great faith. It is better to avoid clichés when it comes to prayer, trouble, illness, suffering. This passage in 2 Cor. 11–12 rules out the superficial and often incorrect answers about life, faith, and prayer.

The paradigmatic prayer that Jesus taught his disciples—what we call the Lord's Prayer but really should be called the Disciple's Prayer—raises some important questions and provides some important clues at key points. For example, it starts by addressing God properly as "Abba, Father" (just as Jesus did in the garden of Gethsemane in Mark 14:36), then continues as a prayer of praise ("Hallowed be thy name"), and a request that God's kingdom and will be done on earth as in heaven, which of course implies that God's will is not yet being perfectly done on earth as it is in heaven. Then we have the intercession asking for daily bread, and notice that there is nothing in this prayer that suggests we should pray for things that are not necessities in life. Next we have the penitential "Forgive us our trespasses/debts," which makes clear that even disciples are not perfect, and indeed regularly sin in some ways (even if it is just sins of omission, such as failing to love one's neighbor as oneself, or failing to love one's enemy) and need to ask for forgiveness. And Jesus connects our receiving such forgiveness with our willingness to practice forgiveness of others when we have been wronged.

The next line of the Lord's Prayer is, however, regularly badly translated and often misunderstood. As James 1:12–16 makes perfectly clear, God cannot be tempted and God tempts no one. Why then the translation "Lead us not into temptation" as a petition directed to God? Actually, what the translation should be is "Do not put us to the test," followed by "Deliver us from the Evil One." By definition, God tests us, but the devil tempts us. A test is meant to strengthen one's character, whereas a temptation is meant to destroy one's moral fiber and character. So, we would be wise to stop asking God not to tempt us, which God doesn't do, and instead ask God not to put us to the test. God and the devil have opposite aims when it comes to human character and human salvation. It is possible that the same circumstance or event can be a test from God if responded to properly, or a temptation from Satan if not. Although God and Satan are not working together, but rather are at odds with each other and what they seek to accomplish with human beings, they can use the same things to accomplish different outcomes. If we can manage to understand and get the Lord's Prayer right, we will be on our way to better discipleship to the Lord who taught us this prayer.

Argument Three, Part Three

Parting Shots

[12:11]I have been a fool. You compelled me to it. You ought to have commended me, since I am not in any way inferior to those "superlative apostles," even if I am nothing. [12]The signs of an apostle were performed among you with all endurance, including signs, and wonders, and miracles. [13]So in what way are you worse off than the other assemblies, except that I did not burden you? Forgive me this wrong!

[14]Look, I am ready to come to you this third time. [Again] I will not burden you, since I am not seeking what is yours, but you. For children ought not to save up for their parents, but rather parents for their children. [15]I will most gladly spend and be spent for you. If I love you more, am I to be loved less? [16]Now granted, I did not burden you, but crafty as I was, by deceit I took you in. [17]Did I take advantage of you by any of those I sent to you? [18]I urged Titus to go and I sent the brother with him. Titus didn't take advantage of you, did he? Didn't we walk in the same spirit and in the same footsteps?

[19]Have you been thinking all along that we have been defending ourselves to you? Before God we are speaking in Christ, and everything, beloved, is for your building up. [20]For I'm afraid that perhaps when I come, I will not find you to be what I want, and you may not find me to be what you want. Perhaps there will be quarreling, jealousy, angry outbursts, selfish ambition, slander, gossip, arrogance, and disorder. [21]I fear that when I come, my God will again humble me in your presence,

> and I will be grieved over many who have sinned earlier and have not repented of the impurity, sexual sin, and debauchery in which they have indulged.
>
> ¹³:¹Yes, this is the third time I am coming to you, [and] "Everything must be determined by the testimony of two or three witnesses." ²I warned when I was there the second time, and now I warn being absent to those who sinned and all the rest—if I come again, I will not be lenient, ³since you seek proof of Christ speaking in me, who is not weak in dealing with you, but powerful among you. ⁴For he was crucified in weakness, but he lives by the power of God.

The danger for modern people reading Paul's fool's discourse is that they may think that this was a form of entertainment, like a clown or a medieval jester. My grandmother, who loved watching Flip Wilson when he had a TV show from 1970 to 1974, used to say after dinner, "Let's go watch Flip Wilson play the fool." And, of course, he did. Whenever he got in a tight spot, he would say, "The devil made me do it." What Paul has done in his fool's discourse is meant to be not entertainment but rather chastisement, a shaming of those who embraced false values and false evaluations of what counted as glory, what counted as being a truly "spiritual superhero."

In a rhetorical discourse like this one, if one's boast is compelled by the audience or the situation, then the handbook says that it's justified for the orator to do it (Quintilian, *Institutio oratoria* 11.1.17–19; Cicero, *Epistulae ad familiares* 5.12.8). Paul lays the credit or blame for this fool's discourse at the feet of his audience, saying, **You compelled me to it**. It's not that they urged Paul to boast; rather, it's that their behavior, being enthralled with the "super-apostles" and their rhetoric, compelled the apostle to respond.

Paul has spoken ironically, sarcastically, tongue in cheek in his bragging, and notice that he has actually not referred to **signs, and wonders, and miracles** until now. He reminds the Corinthians that when he first came to them, the marks of an apostle—signs and wonders and miracles—had been seen in him by them. Are we meant to distinguish these three things with signs referring to acts, events that point beyond themselves, miracles that evoke awe, and healings (cf. Heb. 2:3–4)? It is possible, but Paul does not say. Although we do have some record of Paul performing healings, and perhaps even raising someone from death in the case of Eutychus (see Acts 13:11; 14:9–10; 16:16–18; 19:11–12; 20:7–12), in the whole of Paul's Corinthian correspondence he has not highlighted such things, and even here, when push has come to shove, he mentions it only in passing. In any case, as the list of callings and gifts in 1 Cor. 12:28–30 suggests, others in the faith could also perform miracles, and such persons are distinguished from apostles in the list. In fact, Paul says that he was forced by the Corinthians to do the fool's discourse, never mind remind them in detail about miracles while he was with them.

We would love to know what signs, wonders, and miracles Paul performed while he was in Corinth for about a year and a half, but he doesn't tell us, probably because many in his audience already knew (cf. Rom. 15:19; 1 Cor. 12:28; Gal. 3:5). Those things alone that the Corinthians could bear witness to should have once and for all validated that Paul was a real apostle, indeed was *their* apostle, but unfortunately, like many moderns, the Corinthians seem to have rolled with "The latest is the greatest, and the newest is the truest." So, Paul has to paddle upstream to get them back to a place where they have a good relationship with their founder. It should be noticed that what Paul does not mention as signs of an apostle are the recounting of lavish revelations in detail and the use of Sophistic rhetoric for the purpose of impressing the audience with verbal pyrotechnics.

Preachers take note. You can't impress people into the kingdom of God by your rhetoric. Signs and wonders and miracles are the work of the Spirit, and they occur not in order to impress people but rather to save them, to heal them, to free them. They are not bullet points on a resume to which a preacher could point and say, "Look at what I've achieved!" Although Paul is not trying to inculcate a persecution complex for himself or his coworkers like Timothy and Titus, it is true nonetheless that since we live in a fallen world, if you are doing ministry right, being a humble servant of the Lord and not a self-serving egomaniac, you can count on getting pushback; indeed, you may even encounter abuse and suffering as Paul did.

Paul says, **I will not burden you, since I am not seeking what is yours, but you**. That is, he doesn't want something *from* them; he just wants *them*, a loving relationship with them. This brings to my mind an experience I had while visiting Fourth Presbyterian Church in Bethesda, Maryland, where my college roommate attended. At the time, this church was pastored by Dr. Richard Halverson, a dynamic preacher and minister who also became chaplain to the United States Senate. He told the story of a wealthy parishioner, Charlie, who was very charitable to good causes, lots of them. Halverson called him one day and said he'd like to have lunch with him, and Charlie readily obliged. They had a nice lunch at a nice restaurant, and then Charlie pushed back from the table, expecting a "pitch" from Halverson, and said, "What do you want from me, Pastor?" Charlie was so used to being hit up for money that he figured, "Here it comes again." But Halverson surprised him: "Charlie, I don't want anything from you. I just want you. I just wanted some fellowship time with you. That's all." Charlie was so surprised by this that he began to weep.

Suspicion can lead to cynicism, but here Paul is reassuring his converts that he doesn't personally want something from them for himself; he just wants a positive, indeed loving, relationship with his converts in Corinth. For some Corinthians this seemed hard to believe after Paul had pushed so hard for the collection for the saints in Jerusalem. They assumed that there must be some kickback in that fund for Paul himself. This is why Paul stresses the roles of the legates from each church who will handle the contributions and make sure that they don't get into the wrong hands, including not into Paul's hands.[1]

When Paul says in 12:13 to the Corinthians, **I did not burden you**, he is in fact emphatic about it: the Greek reads, "*I myself* was never a burden." He intends to keep it that way. He draws an analogy with how parents should spend and be spent for their children, not the reverse. Paul clearly has apprehensions about how he will be received when he gets to Corinth for the third time. He has a flashback to his second and painful visit, when he had to leave abruptly because his reception was so negative.

Sometimes we almost forget that Paul was a human being, with feelings just like us, but we see him in a very human moment when he says in 12:21, **I fear that when I come, my God will again humble me in your presence, and I will be grieved over many who have sinned earlier and have not repented**. Here we see a genuine pastoral moment. Paul can't stand the thought of some of his converts not repenting of their sin, and thus ruining their relationship not just with him but also with the Lord. Paul doesn't want to have to mourn the loss of some converts when he shows up, which here he calls a "humbling," but we would likely say that Paul is feeling as if he has failed with those sinners.

Leaders must have enough courage to confront sin and lead people to repentance. It may cost them personally in terms of losing a cordial relationship with a person or persons, but Paul is willing to take that risk. In Paul's day expulsion would have more of an effect because his congregation probably was the only Christian option in town, whereas if we use that means of discipline now, people will just leave, go down the street, and join a different church, as there is rarely any cooperation between churches today about such confidential matters, especially if they are of different denominations.

Here Paul is hoping that this letter has sufficed to wake up the sinners, get them to repent, so that when he comes for the third time, he will not need to exercise church discipline. Remember how Paul told the Corinthians in 1 Cor. 5:1–5 that they needed to exercise discipline and cast out the member who was committing a type of sexual immorality that even pagans found appalling. He

1. See Keener, *1–2 Corinthians*, 240–43.

doesn't want to come to Corinth with a big stick and have to do the painful task of discipline. Even though he is reluctant, he will do it if necessary. Notice that he stresses the sins of the tongue in 2 Cor. 12:20 and then sexual sins in 12:21. Even if this warning against sin doesn't sound familiar, it should, given that we live in the age of social media and in an overly sexualized culture. Those two types of sins are more likely to divide a congregation than almost anything else. Notice that Paul is dealing with ethical, not primarily theological, problems in this case in Corinth.

A word of caution is in order at this point. While it is important for pastors to address problems that they find in their congregation, pastors today can get themselves into a world of trouble by trying to minister to people beyond their training or gifts. Most pastors, even with a master of divinity degree, have had only enough counseling training to spot a complex problem, not to solve it. They should refer persons with deep problems to Christian counselors. Time and again pastors have become enmeshed in sinful situations with their parishioners because they are in over their heads, and they themselves are emotionally needy and vulnerable, and the end result is that they are expelled or are forced to leave the ministry. I have seen this happen again and again. Paul, it appears to me, was wise to write to his congregation about the problems prior to his third visit, and also previously in 1 Cor. 5. He was hoping for a reconciling and reasonably stress-free visit when he came.

Second Corinthians 13:1–4 brings this argument to a close. Paul says that his coming soon will be his third trip to Corinth (something already mentioned in 2 Cor. 12 as a third visit), which transpired in the mid-50s. Little did he know that it would likely be his last one.

Some have thought it odd that Paul quotes Deut. 19:15 (cf. Deut. 17:6; Num. 35:30) at the outset of his announcing this third visit to Corinth: **Everything must be determined by the testimony of two or three witnesses**. As David Garland points out, it is anything but odd if in fact Paul is threatening to act against the sinners or even the so-called super-apostles when he comes. He intends to call witnesses and put them on trial.[2] This, however, is not just an idle threat, for Paul has the apostolic authority to do it. The real issue is not whether Christ speaks in and through Paul but whether Christ lives in the Corinthians, as evidenced by the fruit of the Spirit, among other things. So, Paul will turn the tables on them and tell them that they need to test and authenticate the genuineness of their own faith. It is a fact that only in Old Testament law do we hear that two or three witnesses are required and must agree to validate the truthfulness of any statement or, at the other end of the spectrum, the sin

---

2. See Garland, *2 Corinthians*, 540.

of anyone. Neither Roman nor Greek law sets such a high bar to find someone guilty of something.

It seems clear that Paul and the Corinthians see *exousia* and also *dynamis* in two different ways. The basic meaning of *dynamis* is "power, strength, might," or a "powerful act," such as a miracle. In 1 Cor. 12:28–29 it can refer to a miracle worker, and as a proper noun, "the Power," it can refer to God (Matt. 26:64; Mark 14:62; cf. Acts 8:10). As for *exousia*, it refers to the power to act; hence, a person who has this has authority to act. Authority is established by powerful actions. Thus, for example, Jesus is described as one who has independent authority, as evidenced by his powerful teaching and deeds, and thus is contrasted with the scribes, who have only a derived authority (Matt. 7:29). *Exousia* is the term used to refer to a person who is "under authority" or, by contrast, has authority over others (see Matt. 8:9). "The Corinthians understand power as something exerted by assertive, domineering, forceful personalities who boisterously and tyrannically wield authority. The apostle sees divine power perfected in weakness."[3] Paul also sees his power to perform "mighty works" as derived from the Power—God in Christ—and so he must act in accord with the one who empowered him, and also in accord with the character of the one who sent him, Jesus Christ.

The overall tenor of this section is anxiousness. Paul is anxious to go and find the Corinthians mostly in good relationship with him. He is anxious to deal with the troublemakers, but he'd prefer that they repent before he gets there so that he doesn't have to act as judge and jury for some of them. He keeps hammering home his integral connection with the Corinthians. If they call into question his faith and leadership, well, they are calling into question their own faith, since they were converted through Paul's ministry.

3. Garland, *2 Corinthians*, 544.

The Peroration

The Defense Rests

13:5Test yourselves to see if you are in the faith. [Closely] examine your-selves. Or do you yourselves not realize Christ is within you? Unless you fail the test. ⁶And I am hoping you will realize that we ourselves do not fail the test. ⁷But we pray to God that you do nothing wrong, not that we may appear to pass the test, but that you may do what is right, even though we may appear to fail. ⁸For we are unable to do anything against the truth, but only for the truth. ⁹We rejoice when we are weak and you are strong. We pray that you become mature. ¹⁰This is why I am writing these things while I am absent, so that when I am there, I won't have to deal harshly with you in keeping with the authority the Lord gave me for building you up and not for tearing you down.

A peroration can take several different forms: a listing and recapitulation of the main topics of the discourse, an amplification of the last argument, or just a full-on appeal to the deeper emotions. Paul decides to focus on a particular issue already raised, that of testing: the Corinthians have been really testing Paul—testing his patience, testing his loyalty, testing his rhetorical ability, test-ing his honesty, and much more.

> Paul plays on the verb "to prove" (*dokimazō*, 13:5; see 8:9, 25) and the adjectives "proven" ("approved," *dokimos*, 13:7; see 10:18) and "unproven" ("fail the proof," "unapproved," "counterfeit," *adokimos*, 13:5, 6, 7). He tells the Galatians that each

one should test (*dokimazō*) his own work, then he might have a boast, but only in himself, not by comparing himself to someone else (Gal 6:4). . . . He tells the Corinthians that he beats his body to make it his slave "so that after I have preached to others, I myself will not be disqualified (*adokimos*) for the prize," to warn them that no one can slide by God's judgment (1 Cor 9:27; see 3:13).[1]

Of course, Paul's passing the test and the Corinthians doing so are intertwined, for if the Corinthians fail the test, then Paul has failed in his role as apostle to them to convert them to Christ.[2] This is one reason why Paul is so anxious about their behavior and faith. Paul hopes that on the day of judgment they will boast about their apostle, and vice versa (2 Cor. 1:13b–14).

He says, and wants to say, **Christ is within you**, for he wants to believe the best about his spiritual children; but he has doubts, so he adds, **Unless you fail the test**. The apostle is clearly unsettled, and he wants to get to Corinth and settle various matters and resolve the remaining difficulties. In any case, Paul reminds us that appearances may not be the same as reality. Paul, in his weakness, may appear to fail, but then God's power paradoxically is made perfect in Paul's weakness, so it becomes obvious that it came from beyond Paul, from God's Spirit. Not surprisingly in a defense speech, there is much talk of proof (cf. 2:9; 8:3; 9:13; rarely in his other letters), but now Paul turns the table on his converts.

He's shown his proof of authenticity (see above on the signs of the apostles) again and again, and now, in the end, the Corinthians need to do a reality check—they need to test themselves before Paul gets there, to see if they are bona fide Christians. What ultimately is at stake is whether Paul and his converts will pass the test when they all appear before the judgment seat of Christ for a review of all their deeds (2 Cor. 5:10). This event will transpire when Christ returns to judge the earth (cf. 1 Cor. 3:13). Paul is perfectly content to appear and be weak, if only his converts will be strong and mature in the faith and Christian living.

In 13:8 Paul reveals something fundamental about himself: he cannot act **against the truth**; he must act on behalf of **the truth**. In this case he is talking about the truth of the gospel and the need for at least some of his converts to repent. Paul is so grounded in the truth of the gospel that it has sunk into the very core of his being (see 11:10) such that not only has he no will to act against the truth, but he also has no desire to do so. The love and the truth of Christ compel him to act in a certain way, and in this case it means that he cannot stand idly by and ignore his spiritual children's lies and sins. He must correct them. Sometimes pastors are apt to take the easy way out and ignore sin in

---

1. Garland, *2 Corinthians*, 545.
2. Harris, *Second Epistle to the Corinthians*, 924.

their congregations. But almost always this leads to problems later on. We are not called to be people pleasers but rather are called to embrace the truth of Christ and please God.[3]

The function of this discourse was a ground-clearing exercise, so that when Paul gets to Corinth again, he won't have to be bold, or judge anyone, or have to deconstruct something or someone, in order to build up the congregation as a whole. Paul has been on the defensive in this discourse, but here at the end he warns the audience that *now* it's time for them to test themselves and the genuineness of their faith and their commitment to their original apostle as opposed to the cheap imitations currently bewitching them. "In the logic of the argument, the greater the affirmation of the Corinthians' provenness, the more undeniable Paul's provenness."[4] To judge by the fact that he writes the Letter to the Romans from the port city of Corinth, Cenchreae, perhaps a year or so after 2 Corinthians, it would appear that he got there, stayed a good while, and did sort things out. Or does his staying in the eastern port and not in Corinth itself suggest another, less favorable conclusion? I will say more about this in a moment.

3. See Guthrie, *2 Corinthians*, 642–43.

4. Harris, *Second Epistle to the Corinthians*, 921, quoting from an earlier study by Judith Gundry-Volf. He rightly notes that Paul advances the argument here by rhetorical questions, which require the answer yes in some cases as here (13:5), and no if they begin with the particle *mē* ("not").

Closing Remarks, Greetings, Benediction

> ¹³:¹¹Finally, brothers and sisters, rejoice, become mature, be encouraged, be of the same mind, be at peace, and the God of love and peace *will* be with you. ¹²Greet one another with a holy kiss. ¹³All the saints send you greetings. ¹⁴The grace of the Lord Jesus Christ, and the love of God, and the sharing in common of the Holy Spirit [be] with you all.

The final exhortation in 13:11 is precisely what we would expect for a fractured and factious group of believers. In some ways, this closing would have suited the end of 1 Corinthians just as well as here, for that earlier letter was all about opposing divisions and factions and being united as a body of Christ. It would also suit the situation in Rome, as Rom. 15:5 shows. It is also clear from this closing that the Corinthians still need to hear that exhortation and grow up. They need to be of one mind on the important things, and if they can be at peace with one another, then, Paul promises, the God of love and peace will be with them. Although the word *chairō* can simply mean "farewell," Paul in 13:11 uses it to mean **rejoice**, and as David Garland points out, 1 Thess. 5:16 provides a good parallel, where the word "rejoice" heads a list of final imperatives.[1]

Unlike Rom. 16, where there is a long greeting card with many names at the end, here Paul simply says, **All the saints** [*hagioi*] **send you greetings**. This could be a final reminder that the Jerusalem assembly of believers is part of the same

---

1. Garland, *2 Corinthians*, 552.

faith, and a reminder about the collection for them, or Paul could be using the term *hagioi* ("holy ones") in a more generic way.

On the **holy** or chaste **kiss** on the cheek, we may compare Rom. 16:16; 1 Cor. 16:20; 1 Thess. 5:26; 1 Pet. 5:14. Since it does not occur elsewhere, the adjective "holy" appended to the exhortation to greet with a kiss may be distinctively Pauline.[2] The use of "family" language for the family of faith is ubiquitous in Paul's letters, and this is because Paul, like Jesus in texts like Mark 3:31–35, sees that in the eschatological age the primary family that everyone—single, married, parents, children—needs to be part of is the family of Christian faith. Paul's primary goal is to help create and build up the family of faith, based not on ethnicity, or social status, or wealth, or ancestry, or place of origin, but on being a new creature in Christ joined to the body of Christ by the Holy Spirit. And like all true families, love and affection, and indeed all the fruits of the Spirit, are to be manifested within the community. Tertullian, writing in the late second century, notes how pagans noticed the love that existed within the Christian community: "'Look,' they [non-Christians] say, 'how they [Christians] love one another' (for they themselves hate one another); 'and how they are ready to die for each other' (for they themselves are readier to kill each other)" (*Apology* 39.7).[3]

The holy kiss was adapted and adopted from the practice of hosts greeting their guests this way as they entered a host's home. This is not surprising, since, of course, the earliest Christian meetings were in homes, and customs of hospitality easily transferred over into the assembly meetings. There would be greetings and meals, including the Lord's Supper in the context of a normal meal, as 1 Cor. 11:17–34 makes clear, and Paul really expected his converts to treat one another as more than just friends—rather, as family, with Paul being the spiritual parent of all his converts.

Of course, no one could read this letter and not realize that there is trouble on the home front. The Corinthians were acting more like dysfunctional, immature children, or even spoiled brats in need of some discipline, than like mature Christians. But Paul would much rather persuade his audience to behave like a loving family than have to come to them with the rod of discipline. Nonetheless, he has plenty of references to the latter in this whole discourse. And while we might have hoped for much better after this letter, and after Paul's third visit, perhaps there is a reason why we hear about Paul staying at the eastern port of Cenchreae in the house of the deacon Phoebe rather than at the house of a Christian family right in town, say, that of Stephanas. Even later, when we read

2. See Guthrie, *2 Corinthians*, 652.
3. Author's translation.

the letter of Clement to the Corinthians, called 1 Clement, written probably in the late 90s, we find the Corinthians still struggling with some of the same issues, which Clement of Rome will correct in the same way Paul did forty years earlier! The more things change, the more they stay the same.

The church consists of imperfect people, which is not to say that a congregation cannot become more mature and wiser in the faith, but there will always be problems and challenges. This is all the more the case because Christian meetings then and usually now are not like guild or secret-society meetings. They are deliberately open to the public, because in Paul's day this was an evangelistic movement that also did discipleship, whereas today the church is a discipleship operation that also has a missions committee and evangelistic and revival services. There is an enormous difference between the former and the latter. In fact, in some places the church has degenerated into being primarily a nurture organization for the physical family units (which is what people often mean by a "family church") rather than primarily *being* a family for one and all in the congregation. The latter is what Paul is trying to inculcate in 2 Corinthians.

If we were to assess Paul's problem children known as the Corinthian congregation, we would say that they were spiritually gifted but still too worldly in character, and not as well grounded as they should have been in the Word, which is why Paul in this letter keeps quoting and expositing Scripture at regular intervals. As we noted at the beginning of this study, the Spirit without the Word is like wine without any container to preserve it and give it definite shape, but the Word without the Spirit can be like wineskins with no wine. Paul wants his audience neither to quench the Spirit nor to reject the admonitions of the Word. Neither Spirit nor Word is sufficient, and Paul's mission is to give more scriptural order and shape to the chaos in Corinth without quenching the Spirit. It was a hard balance to strike then, and it is still so today. May God use his Word not just to stir up our spiritual gifts but to give us concrete guidance as to how to use them so that the body of Christ is built up, not divided and torn down.

The final line of the letter is by now a famous benediction. This is the only place in the New Testament where the three members of the Trinity are explicitly mentioned together in such a benediction. A benediction by definition is a good word said over the congregation conveying blessings from God. This is the opposite of a doxology or glory word, which involves the praising of God. So, these two liturgical phrases are pointed in opposite directions, one from God to us, and the other the reverse. If we compare this to elsewhere in Paul's letters, we see that Paul can predicate grace of God (1 Cor. 1:4), love of Christ (2 Cor. 5:14), *koinōnia* of Christ (1 Cor. 1:9).[4]

---

4. Harris, *Second Epistle to the Corinthians*, 938.

As N. T. Wright points out, outside of the biblical tradition, people in Paul's world were not talking about a God of love or the love of God for humankind. You'd be hard pressed to find passages about Zeus or Poseidon or Apollo or Ares or Artemis or their Roman equivalents where these gods are said to have some sort of enduring and profound unconditional love for human beings.[5] Equally surprising is that the grace of Christ is mentioned first in Paul's benediction, but, of course, the audience would not know or experience the love of God if there had not first been **the grace of the Lord Jesus**, who came and died for their sins.

And notice especially the last phrase of Paul's benediction: **the sharing in common** [*koinōnia*] **of the Holy Spirit**. As I said in the discussion of 6:14, "fellowship" doesn't quite capture the meaning of the word *koinōnia*. It refers to sharing something in common with someone or participating in something with someone else, which can result in fellowship. In this case, what the Corinthians are **sharing in common** or participating in in common is **the Holy Spirit**. Despite all the problems occasioned by the misuse of spiritual gifts in Corinth and all the anxiety that this has caused Paul, he has no desire to quench the Spirit; but what he does want is for the Spirit to bind this factious bunch together, while grace and love are being poured into them. Fellowship is what we work out together with the Spirit's leading while the Father and the Son are pouring love and grace into us. But even given all the work of the Trinity, there is still the responsibility of believers to respond as individuals, and also to collectively respond, saying or singing, "We are one in the Spirit; we are one in the Lord; And we pray that all unity may one day be restored."[6]

5. Wright, *Paul for Everyone: 2 Corinthians*, 146–48.
6. Peter Scholtes, "We Are One in the Spirit," in *Hymns of Faith and Life* (Winona Lake, IN: Light and Life, 1976), no. 477.

Bibliography

Adewuya, J. Ayodeji. *Holiness in the Letters of Paul: The Necessary Response to the Gospel.* Eugene, OR: Cascade Books, 2016.

Barclay, John M. G. *Paul and the Gift.* Grand Rapids: Eerdmans, 2017.

———. "Thessalonica and Corinth: Social Contrasts in Pauline Christianity." *Journal for the Study of the New Testament* 47 (1992): 49–74.

Christian, Timothy. *Paul and the Rhetoric of Resurrection: 1 Corinthians 15 as* Insinuatio. Biblical Interpretation Series 205. Leiden: Brill, 2023.

Endean, Deborah L. "A Theological and Exegetical Study of *ḥādāš* with Special Emphasis on Isaiah 40–48." PhD diss., Asbury Theological Seminary, 2021.

Fee, Gordon D. *God's Empowering Presence: The Holy Spirit in the Letters of Paul.* Grand Rapids: Baker Academic, 2011.

Garland, David E. *2 Corinthians.* New American Commentary 29. Nashville: Broadman & Holman, 1999.

Guthrie, George H. *2 Corinthians.* Baker Exegetical Commentary on the New Testament. Grand Rapids: Baker Academic, 2015.

Harris, Murray J. *The Second Epistle to the Corinthians: A Commentary on the Greek Text.* New International Greek Testament Commentary. Grand Rapids: Eerdmans, 2005.

Hodge, Charles. *A Commentary on the Second Epistle to the Corinthians.* Grand Rapids: Eerdmans, 1994.

Hooker, Morna D. "From God's Faithfulness to Ours: Another Look at 2 Corinthians 1:17–24." In *Paul and the Corinthians: Studies on a Community in Conflict; Essays in Honour of Margaret Thrall,* edited by Trevor J. Burke and J. K. Elliot, 233–39. Supplements to Novum Testamentum 109. Leiden: Brill, 2003.

Keener, Craig S. *1–2 Corinthians.* New Cambridge Bible Commentary. Cambridge: Cambridge University Press, 2005.

Kennedy, George. *New Testament Interpretation through Rhetorical Criticism*. Studies in Religion. Chapel Hill: University of North Carolina Press, 1984.

Kruse, Colin. *2 Corinthians*. Exegetical Guide to the Greek New Testament. Nashville: B&H Academic, 2020.

Land, Christopher D. *The Integrity of 2 Corinthians and Paul's Aggravating Absence*. New Testament Monographs 36. Sheffield: Sheffield Phoenix, 2015.

Lightfoot, J. B. *The Epistles of 2 Corinthians and 1 Peter: Newly Discovered Commentaries*. Edited by Ben Witherington III and Todd D. Still. Lightfoot Legacy Set 3. Downers Grove, IL: IVP Academic, 2016.

Long, Fredrick J. *Ancient Rhetoric and Paul's Apology: The Compositional Unity of 2 Corinthians*. Society for New Testament Studies Monograph Series 131. Cambridge: Cambridge University Press, 2004.

———. *II Corinthians: A Handbook on the Greek Text*. Baylor Handbook on the Greek New Testament. Waco: Baylor University Press, 2015.

Martin, Ralph P. *2 Corinthians*. 2nd ed. Word Biblical Commentary 40. Grand Rapids: Zondervan, 2014.

Matera, Frank J. *II Corinthians: A Commentary*. New Testament Library. Louisville: Westminster John Knox, 2003.

Niebuhr, H. Richard. *The Kingdom of God in America*. Middletown, CT: Wesleyan University Press, 1988.

Oropeza, B. J. *Exploring Second Corinthians: Death and Life, Hardship and Rivalry*. Rhetoric of Religious Antiquity 3. Atlanta: SBL Press, 2016.

Philip, Finny. *The Origins of Pauline Pneumatology: The Eschatological Bestowal of the Spirit upon Gentiles in Judaism and in the Early Development of Paul's Theology*. Wissenschaftliche Untersuchungen zum Neuen Testament 2/194. Tübingen: Mohr Siebeck, 2005.

Stark, Rodney. *The Rise of Christianity: A Sociologist Reconsiders History*. Princeton: Princeton University Press, 1996.

Thrall, Margaret E. *A Critical and Exegetical Commentary on the Second Epistle to the Corinthians*. 2 vols. International Critical Commentary. London: T&T Clark International, 1994–2004.

Vasser, Donald Murray. "Slaves in the Christian Household: The Colossian and Ephesian *Haustafeln* in Context." PhD diss., Asbury Theological Seminary, 2020.

Vegge, Ivar. *2 Corinthians, a Letter about Reconciliation: A Psychagogical, Epistolographical, and Rhetorical Analysis*. Wissenschaftliche Untersuchungen zum Neuen Testament 2/239. Tübingen: Mohr Siebeck, 2008.

Welborn, L. L. *An End to Enmity: Paul and the "Wrongdoer" of Second Corinthians*. Beihefte zur Zeitschrift für die neutestamentliche Wissenschaft und die Kunde der älteren Kirche 185. Berlin: de Gruyter, 2011.

Winter, Bruce W. *Philo and Paul among the Sophists*. 2nd ed. Grand Rapids: Eerdmans, 2002.

Witherington, Ben, III. *The Acts of the Apostles: A Socio-rhetorical Commentary*. Grand Rapids: Eerdmans, 1998.

———. *Biblical Theology: The Convergence of the Canon*. Cambridge: Cambridge University Press, 2019.

———. *Conflict and Community in Corinth: A Socio-rhetorical Commentary on 1 and 2 Corinthians*. Grand Rapids: Eerdmans, 1995.

———. *Jesus and Money: A Guide for Times of Financial Crisis*. Grand Rapids: Brazos, 2012.

———. *Jesus the Sage: The Pilgrimage of Wisdom*. Minneapolis: Fortress, 1994.

———. *Letters and Homilies for Jewish Christians: A Socio-rhetorical Commentary on Hebrews, James and Jude*. Downers Grove, IL: IVP Academic, 2007.

———. *The Paul Quest: The Renewed Search for the Jew of Tarsus*. Downers Grove, IL: InterVarsity, 1998.

———. *Paul's Letter to the Romans: A Socio-rhetorical Commentary*. With Darlene Hyatt. Grand Rapids: Eerdmans, 2004.

———. *Sola Scriptura: Scripture's Final Authority in the Modern World*. Waco: Baylor University Press, 2023.

———. *Troubled Waters: The Real New Testament Theology of Baptism*. Waco: Baylor University Press, 2007.

———. *A Week in the Life of Corinth*. Downers Grove, IL: IVP Academic, 2012.

Witherington, Ben, III, and Jason A. Myers. *Paul of Arabia: The Hidden Years of the Apostle to the Gentiles*. Eugene, OR: Cascade Books, 2022.

Wright, N. T. *Paul for Everyone: 2 Corinthians*. 2nd ed. New Testament for Everyone. Louisville: Westminster John Knox, 2004.

Index of Authors

Index of Scripture
and Other Ancient Writings

31:31–34 46
32:38 82

Lamentations

4:2 62

Ezekiel

1 125
11:19 48
20:34 82
20:41 81
23:5–8 114
36:26 48
37:27 81, 82

Daniel

7:13–14 57, 125
12:1–3 61

Hosea

1:1–2:2 114
8:7 99

Amos

5 99

Zechariah

8:20–23 95

Old Testament Apocrypha

2 Maccabees

1:5 70
5:20 70
7:33 70
8:29 70

Sirach

7:3 99

Wisdom of Solomon

7:14 55
7:26 55, 56

New Testament

Matthew

4:24 66
6:33 76
7:29 134
8:9 134
8:10–11 95
9:22 68
25:40 21
26:64 134

Mark

3:31–35 140
12:41–44 102
14:36 127
14:62 134

Luke

4:38 66
8:37 66
8:45 66
12:50 66
19:43 66
21:1–4 102
22:63 66
23:34 21
23:43 122
23:46 53

John

14–17 31
14:2 58
14:9 55, 56
14:16 31
16:13 32
3:1–8 69
3:5–8 31
9:1–3 127

Acts

2:1–4 31
2:43–47 100
2:44–45 98
4:32 98
4:32–37 100
6:1–7 93

7:48–50 53, 58
7:57 66
7:58 69
8:10 134
9 21, 23
9:1–19 125
9:4 21
9:23–25 119
13:11 130
14:9–10 130
15 94, 99
15:22–29 80, 86
16:6–10 29
16:16 130
18 5, 16
18:5 66
18:12–17 5
19:11–12 130
20:2–3 2
20:4 95
20:7–12 130
21 95
22 23
22:6–16 125
22:23–30 5
26 23
26:12–18 125
28:8 66

Romans

1 47
1:3–4 57
4:8 116
5:10 70
5:12–21 48
5:19 71
6:1–14 32
6:19 81
7:12 45
8:1–2 70
8:1–4 48
8:13 23
8:28 55
8:28–30 56
8:38–39 68
9–11 14
10:9 57
11:26 14, 58
12:2 80